HOW TO MAKE SUCCESSFUL DECISIONS

HOW TO MAKE SUCCESSFUL DECISIONS

For University Students

D. Amalor

KALPAZ

How to Make Successful Decisions:
For University Students

ISBN : 978-81-7835-926-7

Published in 2012 in India by
Kalpaz Publications
C-30, Satyawati Nagar,
Delhi - 110052
E-mail: kalpaz@hotmail.com
Ph.: 9212729499

Laser Type Setting : Rajender Vashist, Delhi
Printed at : Chawla Offset Printers, Delhi

Dedicated to
My father ***Divianadane,***
my mother ***Andoniammalle***
and my elder brother ***D. Jile***
who taught me primary school lessons

Contents

Foreword

In the context of globalisation, life is becoming increasingly complex. Hence on one side, there is information overload and on the other the experiences of the earlier generations cannot always guide the future. In such a context, there is a demand to rely on one's own decision making skills. In any life situation, one is faced with a multitude of alternatives. Choosing the right one involves judicious use of information. Only relevant experience or timely counselling can help.

The central element in decision making is the decision maker. The decision maker's characteristics can influence the quality of the decision which in turn has an impact on the quality of the life of the person. Dr. D. Amalor has chosen an area that is socially relevent. We require scientific knowledge to guide people to develop appropriate decision making skills. This book is an attempt in that direction. This book can be useful not only to the professionals in the field but also to any person who wishes to strengthen one's decision making skill.

Dr. V. Suresh
Professor and Head
Psychology Wing
Directorate of Distance Education
Annamalai University.

Preface

With the advent of advancement in communication and information technology, life has become more and more complicated. Nowadays people experience more pscyhological stress than ever before. Multiplicity of alternatives for one course of action could be one of the reasons for the psychological stress. Effective conflict resolution only can give satisfaction and make life meaningful.

Conflict resolution requires deciding the appropriate alternative among the many. People who make right decision can gain satisfaction and who make the wrong decision experience loss, stress, strain. So people must know the ways of making quality decisions.

This book provides some understanding of how people make quality decisions in general and the decision making styles of university students who are going to build the nation tomorrow in particulars.

At this moment I would like to express my sincere thanks to Dr. V. Suresh, M.A., M.Phil., Ph.D. Professor and Head, Psychology Wing, Directorate of Distance Education, Annamalai University who guided and supervised this research work and gave me valuable suggestions and motivation in preparing this document.

I am also thankful to the authorities of Annamalai University for having granted me permission to publish this research work.

D. Amalor

Puducherry,
11-11-2011

List of Figures and Tables

Figures

Tables

1

Introduction

In our day to day life, we face many situations in which we are caught amidst many alternatives for a problem. The individual has to choose one among the alternatives that are at his disposal for a future course of action. The selection of the alternative is the core of decision making. It is the appropriateness of the alternative to the problem that determines the worth of the decision.

Decision making is a cognitive process of analysing various solutions to a particular problem and arriving at a particular solution for a future course of action. So, it becomes clear that when an individual indulges in decision making, the decision is not arrived at all of a sudden. Instead, it involves certain steps or process (Simon *et. al.*, 1966).

PROCESS OF DECISION MAKING

When an individual faces a problem, the first step is appraising the challenge. This involves the time dimension (the duration of the time taken to solve the problem and the distance of the problem etc.) and the consequences of attending to the problem or neglecting it; whether it is a simple one or complex one requiring more time and care and the importance of the problem in the future environment. All these help the individual in giving a clear picture of the situation. Neglecting any of these may lead to a faulty decision. A clear understanding of the problem helps in generating as many alternatives as possible to make a worthy decision based on experience and adequate information. It is only in this phase, when there is a lack of information, the individual identifies a gap in his knowledge. Filling in this gap is essential for decision making.

Once the alternatives are generated, the next task of the individual is to eliminate the inappropriate alternatives and to choose the most appropriate alternative. This involves a careful consideration of merits and demerits of each alternative. It is always desirable to generate as many alternatives as possible, because the more the number of alternatives the better the chances of identifying a better solution to the problem.

After the alternative is chosen, the next task of the individual is to make commitment to put the alternative into action. This mainly involves finding the way for gaining the approval from the other significant people. That is, the individual translates the chosen alternative into a tentative plan of action. The cumulative tension of considering many alternatives can be resolved only by making a commitment. Sometimes the tension may make the individual act impulsively. This spoils the whole process.

When putting the chosen alternative into a course of action, the individual may have to face criticisms. That is, only the demerits are pointed out by others. It should be agreed that any decision involves certain amount of risk. So the individual should be open to valuable criticisms and should not get discouraged by them. Any strategy adopted to make decisions ignoring these steps will lead to faulty decision making.

FACTORS INFLUENCING DECISION MAKING

Newell and Simon (1972) describe three major dimensions along which a human problem solving process can vary, viz. task dimension, individual difference dimension, and performance-learning-development dimension.

The individual difference dimension consists of two factors. One is expertise in the problem domain. It has been found that experts continuously extend and refine their skills to develop an intuition that most novices lack, which is used in solving difficult and complex problems (Larkin, *et. al.*, 1980). The solution strategies used by experts are usually different from novices (Andersen, 1985). This implies that giving training on certain activity or providing a variety of experiences helps an individual in becoming a better decision maker.

The second factor that influence decision making is psychological and personal characteristics. This includes cognitive style, personality and demographic and situational variables (Bariff & Lusk, 1977; Zmud, 1979; Ghani & Lusk, 1982; Blaylock & Rees, 1984). The personality characteristics include locus of control, the level of tolerance to ambiguity, risk taking propensity, extraversion/introversion, n Ach, anxiety level and self-esteem (Lefcourt, 1972; Dermer, 1973; Taylor and Dunnette, 1974; Eysenck, 1967).

1. Locus of Control

Locus of control is an individual's generalised expectancy of the degree of control over what happens to them (Rotter, 1966). On this basis, individuals differ in viewing oneself as either the determiner of one's own fate (Internal locus of control) or as the hapless victim of the external forces (External locus of control). In the former case, the individual presumably expects that there is relatively high probability (P) that his own decisions can lead to the attainment of his goals (subjective expected utility).

On the other hand, a person may become most willing to undertake decision having possibly unpleasant consequences if his own connection with the decisions to take the step is diffused through a group consensus (Bem, Wallach and Kogan, 1965). Thus, the external locus of control has been found to be related to poor achievement behaviour (Coleman, Campbell, Hobson & Mc Partland, 1966), greater conformity (Odel, 1959; Mac Donald, 1972) and positive reaction to influence attempts (Ritchie & Phares, 1969; Biondo & Mac Donald, 1971).

The social learning theory of Rotter (1954) attributes the strength of the tendency to undertake some decision to the strength of the cognitive expectations that the decision will produce certain consequence (p) and the attractiveness (SEU) to the individual. So the individual takes a decision so as to maximize subjectively expected utility (SEU), (Edwards, 1954) where for each alternative activity in a given setting

$$SEU = p1.u1 + p2.u2 + \dots pn.un$$

there are n possible consequences of that particular course of action and the first consequence has utility (u1) and subjective probability (p1) and so on. The latter mathematically represents the strength of expectancy or degree of certainty as probability from 0 to 1.

Guided by this general conception, one begins to

think of the overall strength of a tendency to undertake a particular task or decision of corresponding to SEU. Its strength should be equivalent to the sum of various components of motivational tendencies such as the tendency to achieve success (e.g. corresponding to p1.u1) plus the tendency to gain approval (e.g. corresponding to p2.u2) and so on.

2. Need for Achievement

The tendency to achieve success also known as need for achievement (abbreviated n Ach) is competition with a standard of excellence (Mc Clelland, *et. al.* 1953). It involves the concept of expectancy, which refers to the degree of belief that some act will be followed by some consequence (ps) and the concept of incentive value of the expected consequence or goal (Ins/U). These two are the basic building blocks in the kind of theory advanced earlier by Tolman (1955) and Lewin (1938) and by contemporary workers like Rotter (1954) and others in the field of decision making (see Edwards, 1954).

Atkinson (1978) identified one more factor known as motive to success (Ms) to influence the tendency to achieve success. So, at times, when the individual believes his performance is dependent upon his own skill (i.e. internal locus of control) the tendency to achieve success (Ts) is a multiplicative product of Ms, Ps and Ins. Mathematically,

$$Ts = Ms \times Ps \times Ins$$

Where Ms refers to the motive to success, Ps refers to probability of success and Ins refers to incentive values. The n Achiever should be experienced in maximising payoffs relatively free from anxiety about failure and therefore efficient at those tasks he chooses to attempt (Birney, 1968).

The early works of Escalona (1940), Festinger (1942), Lewin et.al. (1944), Atkinson (1957) and Litwin (1958) proved that in achievement oriented situation (i.e. when motive for success is greater than motive for failure) Ins and Ps are inversely related. That is, Ins=1-Ps. This relationship enables to maximize the value of the expression Ps x Ins. The expression gets its maximum when Ps=0.5 and Ins=0.5. This reasoning enabled Atkinson and Feather (1966) to establish the fact the individuals with high need for achievement to take the decisions of intermediate difficulty.

So, individuals have to lose some alternatives giving high incentive value for want of high probability of occurrence, and some alternatives giving high probability of occurrence for want of high incentive value. In this ambiguous situation, for a better adjustment, the individual is supposed to have some level of tolerance.

3. The Level of Tolerance to Ambiguity

A decision involves subjective expected value (SEU). Generally, in a decision situation, ambiguity is caused by values. Terry (1972) observed that values of the decision maker affect the decision making process. Unless the individual has a clear understanding of his personal values, there will be conflicts between solutions. To reduce ambiguity or to increase the level of tolerance, the individual has to clearly identify the personal values and the problems outside as perceived by him/her. An understanding of this kind will help the individual to generate clear and mutually exclusive alternatives for a particular problem.

Even though the alternatives are generated, the individual has to choose one alternative appropriate to the value system which has its future consequence, not known to that individual and on which the individual has no control or prediction and hence uncertain. Uncertainty is a block in a decision situation. This requires some level of risk taking propensity on the part of the individual.

4. Risk Taking Propensity

Though the decisional outcome is uncertain, an individual has to select one alternative among many. So, decision making involves some level of risk taking propensity. Risk taking propensity is an ambition to deal with the problem in uncertain situation. Blaylock *et. al.* (1984) argued that three factors combine risk perception. The three factors are cognitive style of decision maker, decision environment and traditional risk measure.

Kogan and Wallach (1967) suggest that skill (outcome) contest appear to stimulate a moderate level of risk taking whereas a chance (outcome) context seemed to induce an avoidance of intermediate in favour of extremely risky or conservative strategies. In any given situation, individual usually weighs all the alternative course of action and then makes a decision which (he believes on this basis of his 'self') will maximize pleasure or minimize pain (Lindzey and Aronson, 1954) and according to decision theorists, it has the greatest expected utility (Edwards, 1954).

So, individuals with optimistic characteristic select the alternative that gives a maximum payoff. Pessimistic and conservative people used to select the alternative corresponding to the maximum of the minimum payoff. In the least case, that is, in threatening situations, anxious people consider the situation in terms of losses (Wine, 1971) and they don't want to take risk and select the alternative corresponding to the minimum of the maximum opportunity losses. These rules are called 1. The Maximax criterion 2. Maximini criterion and 3. Minimax criterion rules of mathematical decision theory, respectively.

So, it is clear that a decision making depends upon the individual's thorough understanding of his/ her self in relation to the past experiences and present situation. An understanding of this kind leads to the understanding of the level of self-esteem which influences the decision making process.

5. Self-esteem

"Self-esteem is a learned sense of self based on his perception of the regard he had received from others" (Meador and Rogers, 1973). Coopersmith (1967) found that the environmental sources of high self-esteem are early experiences of success in setting and accomplishing one's goals. Studies suggest that individuals with high, medium and low self-esteem differ in the responses to self-disclosure, and positive feedback (Holstein, Goldstein and Bem, 1971; Mareck and Mettee, 1972). These results suggest the existence of chronic level of self-esteem that is consistent across time.

A good deal of evidence is found from the link between decision making styles and self-esteem as a decision maker by Janis and Mann,(1977) which was confirmed by Burnett *et. al.* (1989) Moore *et. al.*(1990) and Cheryl Ormond *et. al.* (1991).

Individuals with low self esteem tend to be more easily persuaded and prone to conformity to situational demands (Marlowe and Crowne, 1961; Strickland & Crown, 1962; Aronson, 1980), more responsive to social reinforcement under verbal conditioning procedures (Crown & Strickland, 1961 Marlowe, 1962; Marlowe &

Beecher, Cock & Doob, 1964), less likely to express aggression and sometimes more responsive to persuasion and social influence (Berkowitz and Lundy, 1957; Janis and Field, 1959; Lessor and Abelson,1959; Leventhal and Perloe, 1962). Those low in self-esteem deteriorated greatly following failure while the performance of those with high self esteem greatly improved following success (Shrauger and Rosenberg, 1970). This is probably because, persons with low self-esteem were four times more likely than those persons with high self esteem to have unstable self image (Rosenberg, 1965).

Researches by Dittles (1959) and others indicate that persons with low self-esteem are more affected by the evaluative nature of social feedback. They were also more likely to suffer from various psychosomatic symptoms such as anxiety (Howard and Kubis, 1964) which is mediated by uncertainty about a future outcome, would greatly affect the decision making process.

6. Anxiety Level

Anxiety is defined as an emotional state in which there is vague, generalised feeling of fear (Donn Byrne, 1966). It is a learned (Watson and Raynor, 1920) motive to avoid failure (Atkinson and Litwin, 1960; Raynor, 1970) and a concept just opposite to motive for success. Generally when the motive to achieve success is greater than motive for failure, the individual approaches a decision. But on the opposite pattern he/she avoids a decision activity.

Nichols Hoppe et al (1990) found that high anxious subjects inspected more information and more of them were redundant. Students with extremely high level of anxiety may have their performance impaired. They may be so anxious about the possibility of doing poorly in the examination that they are unable to concentrate on their studies. Research has confirmed that students with moderate level of anxiety tend to receive better grades in college than students who have low anxiety levels (Sarason 1957, Suinn 1965).

High levels of anxiety have been found to undermine performance (Sarason 1957). Sarason (1975) suggested that this preoccupation with oneself in terms of worries about one's competence and personal worth on the one hand or feelings of ambivalence about striving to attain externally imposed standards of achievement on the other, may interfere with one's concentration on the task and consequently undermine one's performance.

Spence and Spence (1966) found that anxiety was associated with superior performance of an easy task but an inferior performance of a difficult one. Many studies confirmed the fact that the performance on a task appears to be an inverted 'U' shaped function of activation, or a curvilinear relationship between anxiety and performance. For example, Samuel *et. al.* (1976) and Samuel (1977) found as predicted by Yerks & Dodson (1908); Duffy (1957) Malmo (1959) that anxiety (more generally emotional arousal) at a very high level disrupts performance. When it is very low, it is insufficient to motivate peak performance. It is when anxiety or arousal is at moderate level that the performance is optimal.

Further, the study on the effect of overall strength of a tendency on the level of achievement related performance has provided additional evidence of the curvilinear relationship between motivation and efficiency of performance discovered earlier in other contexts (Yerks & Dodson, 1908; Birch, 1945; Hebb, 1955; Broadhurst; 1959; and Eysenck 1967).

7. Extraversion/Introversion

The personality dimension of extraversion and introversion is based on physiological difference and might hold implication for individual difference in sensation and perception. Extraverts who tend to be outgoing and sociable have a low level of physiological arousal which causes them to be relatively insensitive to external stimulation. Introverts who tend to be more withdrawn and introspective are thought to have high levels of physiological arousal which makes them especially sensitive to internal stimuli (Eysenck, 1967).

Extraverts tend to interpret and make judgments based on the world outside themselves. The attention of the extravert is on people and objects outside themselves. Specific characteristics include an —— "awareness and reliance on the environment for stimulation and guidance; an action oriented, sometimes impulsive way of meeting life; frankness; ease of communication or sociability (Myers and Mc Caulley, 1985).

There also seem to be general individual difference in regard to felt power, which cut across difficult tasks and relationship. A high-power outgoing, confident person generally has a high comparison level (Thibaut and Kelley 1959). According to the present suggestion, these persons would more often be found in problem solving activities. This notion gains support from the works on Internal Locus of control, (Cromwell 1963, Lefcourt 1966, Rotter 1966, Seeman & Evans 1963).

Introverts tend to interpret and make judgments based on the world inside them. Their attention is on ideas and on their perception of those ideas. Specific characteristics include "Interest in clarity of concepts and ideas; reliance on enduring concepts more than on transitory external events, a thoughtful contemplative detachment; and enjoyment of solitude and privacy (Myers & Mc Caulley, 1985).

Thus, it seems that a multitude of factors exert signficant influence on making a decision. Apart from these psychological variables, earlier studies show that various demographic variables such as age, intellectual capacity, experience, education have also been found to influence decision making (Taylor, 1975; Hunt & Lansman, 1975; Taylor & Dunette, 1974).

In the present study psychological variables like extraversion, neuroticism, psychoticism, decision self esteem and achievement motivation and demographic variables like gender, birth order and course of study were included. Attempt has been made to find out the relationship of these variables with decision making styles.

THE NEED FOR THE PRESENT STUDY

Janis and Mann (1977) developed conflict theory of decision making process. Based on Janis and Mann's conflict model, Cheryl Ormond, et al (1991) studied metacognitive analysis of decision making in adolescence using GOFER (Goals, Option, Feedback, Effects, and Review) model of decision making (Mann et.al.,1988). The study revealed a curious (and unwarranted) discrepancy between females' knowledge and performance on decision tasks and self-concept as a decision maker. In order to test this descrepancy in Indian context the present study is conducted.

Also the decision conflict model is of recent origin. We do not have adequate investigations to definitely prove the relationship between the decision coping pattern and the personality and demographic variables. Since an understanding of the relationship among the variables studied has implication for counseling, the present study is conducted.

IMPLICATION OF THE PRESENT STUDY

Any individual indulges in decision making everyday. Many situations or problems may create a conflict in the individual due to uncertainty or many alternatives. In such a conflicting situation it is important that the individual copes with the situation in an effective manner rather than acting impulsively or avoiding the problem. Such defective coping patterns may hinder the development of the individual and may affect his mental and physical health.

One of the factors that influence the decision making style of an individual is personality. Hence self-esteem as a decision maker, Extraversion, Neuroticism, Psychoticism and achievement motivation have been chosen as personality variables for the present study. An understanding of the relationship among these variables has implications for counseling the individuals.

LIMITATIONS OF THE PRESENT STUDY

1. The subjects for the present study were sampled from the students of Annamalai University. So the findings of the study are confined to this population alone.
2. Only final year students (students who are likely to complete their college study) have been chosen for the present study. Students of other strata have not been taken into account.
3. The size of the sample of the present study is small (N=114). A larger sample would give a more reliable result. So it may not be appropriate to generalize the findings.
4. This is only a correlation study. A correlation

coefficient reveals only the nature of relationship between two variables. The cause and effect relationship has not been studied.

5. Rural and Urban differences and the differences in socio-economic status have not been studied.

DEFINITION OF TECHNICAL TERMS

The author of the Flinders Decision Making Questionnaire, (DMQ-I and DMQ-II) Leon Mann (1982) operationally defined the decision making styles as follows:

1. Vigilance (V): is the tendency to search carefully for information, to consider many alternatives, to consider information without bias, and to evaluate alternatives carefully before making a choice.

2. Hyper vigilance / Panic (H): is the tendency to make decisions impulsively and to look for quick, easy solutions to problems.

3. Defensive avoidance (D): is a general tendency to try to avoid or escape from having to make a decision.

4. Rationalisation (R): is the tendency to avoid reality of decisions. This is achieved by ignoring or denying unpleasant aspects of the decision or by concentrating only on the positive aspects of the choice.

5. Buck passing (B): is the tendency to leave the hard decisions to others, to avoid taking responsibility for decisions and to blame others when the decision is wrong.

6. Procrastination (P): is the tendency to put off making decisions by doing other things or by thinking about it for too long.

7. Self esteem as a decision maker: is somewhat

the consistent sense of personal worth in making decisions. In this work the term self esteem refers to self- esteem as a factor contributing to decision making.

The author of the EPQ(R), Eysenck and Eysenck (1975) operationally defined personality and its dimensions as follows:

1. Personality: is more or less stable and enduring organisation of a person's character, temperament, intellect and physique that determines his unique adjustment to his environment.

2. Extraversion: is identified with typical characteristics like 'craving for excitement, taking chance, often sticking one's neck .... out and generally liking change.

3. Neuroticism: is identified with the arousability of the autonomic nervous system. It is characterised by trait anxiety and instability.

4. Psychoticism: is characterised by 11 dispositions.

(a) solidarity, not caring for people.

(b) Troublesome, not fitting in

(c) cruel, inhuman

(d) lack of feeling, insensitive

e) sensation seeking, under aroused

(f) hostile to others, aggressive

(g) like odd and unusual things

(h) disregard danger, foolhardy

(i) like to make fool of other people, upsetting them

(j) opposed to accepted social customs

(k) engaged in little personal interaction, prefer 'impersonal' sex.

5. Need for achievement (n Ach): is a competition with a standard of excellence (Mc Clelland *et. al.* 1953).

2

Review of Literature

The previous chapter dealt with an introduction of the problem, the background and need for the present study. This chapter deals with the earlier investigations that have been done with the variables related to the present study. These investigations have been grouped under two headings viz. studies in general, and specific.

STUDIES IN GENERAL

Studies conducted on personality dimensions and some of its correlates relevant to the present study are reviewed under this heading.

PERSONALITY DIMENSIONS

1. Personality - Characteristics

Studies conducted on extraversion tendency revealed that extraverts have higher threshold for pain (Halsam, 1967) for vision (Siddle,1969) for touch (Coles, 1971) for taste (Eysenck, 1973) and for hearing (Stelmach, 1977). These studies reveal that extraverts are typically under aroused (Eysenck, 1967). In order to bring the arousal up to an optimum level, extraverts would be motivated by and large to increasing stimulation (Eysenck, 1967 and Revelle *et. al.* 1976). Smith Barry *ei. al.* (1990) using 36 male and 36 female extraverted and 36 male 36 female introverted university students found that the regression measure of habitation rate, involving a regression coefficient corrected for the influence of the intercept, showed more rapid habituation in extraverts than in introverts.

Bolgar Nial (1990) tested the proposition that coping is personality in action under stress. The result indicated that neuroticism influences coping efforts and increases in daily anxiety under stress. Two types of coping (1) wishful thinking, and (2) Self blame explained over half the relationship between neuroticism and increases in pre-examination anxiety.

Mc Rae, Robert (1990) reported that individuals high on neuroticism are pronc to worry regardless of presence of threats and prone to feeling of depression even in the absence of loss. It was also reported that neuroticism influences perceptions of stress, and ways of coping.

Studies conducted on psychoticism dimension reveal that psychoticism is a compound measure of (1) anxiety, (2) associative difficulty and (3) suspiciousness, (Singh 1978). Tarrier *et. al.* (1989) found that psychotic subjects were morbidly jealous. Pearson Paul and Sheffield (1989) administered the purpose in life test and the Eysenck personality Questionnaire to 83 young female nurses. Purpose in life was significantly negatively related to psychoticism and Neuroticism and Positively to Extraversion. Result supported the hypothesis that individuals high in Psychoticism tend to have little purpose in life. Tarrier *et. al.* (1989) hypothesised that irrational jealous cognition vary with subjective feelings of insecurity and low self-confidence, in 159 morbidly jealous women. Results showed that morbidly jealous subjects were significantly more introverted neurotic and psychotic than normal subjects.

The characteristics of Extraversion, Neuroticism and Psychoticism dimensions suggest that there must be a relationship between these personality dimensions and decision making styles.

As far as the decision making process is concerned, there is a good deal of evidence both from studies of individuals (Irwin and Smith, 1956; Driscoll and Lanzetta,1964; Long and Ziller, 1965) and of groups (for example Bales, 1950, Zander and Wolfe, 1964) that predecisional information seeking does in fact occur.

The decision maker must utilize various types of information in the decision process. This process has been described by Holis (1969) as personalising information. Studies that revealed a close relationship between the personality dimensions and information processing also confirm that personality is related to decision making process.

For example, Etringer Brucce (1990) found that anxiety and uncertainty over making a choice correlated with a need to gather career related information.

Nicols Hoppe *et. al.* (1990) found that highly anxious subjects inspected more information and more of it was redundant, than did low anxious subjects. The amount of information inspected was influenced by all 3 task variables in addition to anxiety, task complexity and decision importance but not evaluation pressure, as well as anxiety influenced the amount of reinspection (redundancy) of information. Heaton Allen (1991) found that introverts used early information, forming judgments to a significantly greater extent than extraverts when time pressure was high. No significant difference was found between introversion and extraversion when time pressure was low.

Thus, earlier studies reveal a close association between personality and decision making. There were studies to show the relationship of personality with decision making under time pressure. However, there were dearth of studies relating personality with decision making under conflicting situation. Hence the present study.

Though the present study attempts to find out the relationship between decision making styles and personality dimensions, for further understanding, studies conducted on personality dimension in association with some of the other related variables are reviewed in the following pages.

2. Personality Vs n Ach

Heaven Patric (1990) examined the relative importance of a range of personality and attitudinal variables as predictors of n Ach. Result indicated that there is significant negative correlation between impulsiveness (Neuroticism) and n Ach. Ray (1990) in a cross cultural study found that Neuroticism (as measured by EPQ) is essentially irrelevant to n Ach.

Thamson Elzo (1990) examined the relationship between 16PF score and the scores of n Ach. Result indicated that Emotional stability and an Experimental approach were positively correlated with n Ach among males, for females none of the 16 PF factors were correlated with n Ach. Since these studies reveal an inconsistent result, in the present study n Ach is included as a variable.

3. Personality Vs Self - esteem

Raymond (1990) proved Brown's hypothesis that

certain illusion such as unrealistic optimisms as predictably associated with positive affect, social skill and intellectual functioning. The result and significant correlations between confidence ratings and dispositional variables supported the hypothesis. Removing the effects of accuracy suggested that illusory confidence is associated with personality traits that load saliently on factors labeled Affective and Conative / Social. Brown (1990) found that the number and range of negative comments about self seemed to be a most important predictor of subsequent onset of depression.

These studies reveal a close relationship between personality and self-esteem. This relationship implies that decision making self-esteem must also be related to personality. In order to find the nature of relationship, certain additional hypotheses have been formulated and tested in the present study.

4. Personality Dimension Vs Sex

The study of sex difference in personality is receiving more and more attention. The division of societies into age-sex categories is perhaps the features of greatest importance for establishing participation of the individual in culture (Linton, 1945). It is Mussen's (1969) point of view that no other factor exerts more influence on your overt behaviour, your emotional reactions, your cognitive functions, your covert attitudes and your general psychological adjustments than your sex.

Surveys (Carlson, 1971) of two major personality journals (Journal of personality and Social Psychology) as late as 1968 found that there was still a serious imbalance in the sex of subjects used for experiments. But, the most consistent findings on sex difference is that there are really very few sex differences (Maccoby and Jacklin, 1974).

Besides failing to test for sex difference in personality, Carlson (1977) also felt that the field of personality was overlooking an even more significant problem in the psychology of women. Not only were the male subjects the main stay of research problems, but when women were studied, they often studied in terms of male dimensions.

Thus, the research on sex difference in personality dimension is by no means complete. Although Maccoby and Jacklin (1974) provide an exhaustive review, this field is constantly changing (Block 1976). In order to find the present trend on sex difference with regard to personality dimensions, the sample was subdivided on the basis of gender and the data were analysed.

5. Personality Vs Birth Order

George and Abraham (1975) studied the relationship between certain personality traits and birth order among secondary school students. Results indicated that on the factor Extraversion, there is significant difference between birth orders, indicating that middle born have more extraversion tendency. Though not significant, first born have more neuroticism tendency.

Vithal Rao S.Yadav (1988) studied the relationship between birth order and personality dimensions. The study was carried out for a sample of 240 college female adolescents of 17 to 20 years. Personality Dimension was measured by EPI. Result indicated that there is no significant difference in Extraversion dimension with regard to birth order. But there is significant difference in the level of Neuroticism with regard to birth order. The 2nd born and 3rd borns have more Neuroticism tendency than first borns.

These studies reveal a contradictory finding. In order to confirm the fact, one additional objective with regard to birth order has been included in the present study.

ACHIEVEMENT MOTIVATION

1. Achievement Motivation - Characteristics

In general, people with high achievement imagery index score, complete more tasks under achievement orientation, solve more simple arithmetic problems on a timed test, improve tasks in their ability to do anagrams, tend to get better grades, use more future tense and abstract nouns in talking about themselves... and so on (Mc Clelland *et. al.* 1953). French and Thomas (1958) showed that high n Ach subjects would persist longer at trying to solve what (unknown to them) were impossible anagrams.

Mukerji and Sinha (1970) proposed that individuals high in n Ach perceive themselves more positively and hence closer to their ideal self. Rathi (1981) studied the relationship between Locus of control and n Ach. The study was carried out for a sample of 224 male clerks randomly drawn from the central and state Government officers in the age group of 25-32 years. The result showed that Locus of control was found to exert a significant effect upon n Ach: the result also supported the notion that Locus of control is associated with n Ach. The clerks with internal Locus of control were high on n Ach as compared to clerks with external Locus of control.

Ajith K. Dalal and Anitha Sethi (1988) examined the mediating role of attribution. Data pertaining to achievement motivation, causal attribution and performance related consequences (affect and expectancy) have been analyzed. Causal attributions for repeated success and failure by individuals differing in their achievement needs were examined. Undergraduate students of Allahabad University were selected as high need achievers and low need achievers, by administering EPPS.

The students were given anagram tasks on which they either succeeded or failed in all three trials. High need achievers showed an increased tendency in comparison to low need achievers to attribute success to their own efforts and attribute failure to both lack of effort and task difficulty. As predicted by Weiner's (1972) theory, affective responses correlated with internal causes and expectation with stable causes. These linkages were, however, stronger in the case of high need achievers under the failure conditions.

Herrel (1981) found that executives had higher need for power in arriving at decisions, whereas engineers and graduates had higher need for Achievement and Affiliation. Nair (1986) studied the relationship between n Ach and age and Educational level for a sample of 151 officers of business group in a public enterprise (age 25-50 years). The result indicated that there is an inverse relationship between n Ach and age, and there is no relationship between n Ach and different educational levels.

A high level of achievement motivation, furthermore, produces a high level of muscular tension (Muecher and Heckhausen 1962), and possibly also a predisposition to psychosomatic ailments (Rudin, 1964, 1965).

People with strong achievement needs may be highly conformist if they regard conformity as instrumental to achievement (Zajonc and Wahi, 1961). They may also be inclined to cheat on some tasks if this deviant behaviour will bring them achievement rewards and they are relatively unable to postpone their gratifications (Mischel and Gilligan,1964). Thus, we should also recognize that high achievement motivation can be associated with many different conditions, some socially 'good' others 'bad'.

2. Achievement Motivation Vs Self–esteem

Mastery and dissociation are the two major ways in which people deal with threats (Klein, 1971). When a person is threatened, he may face up to the threat in some fashion, master the problem and acquire new competence and self-esteem in this process.

Nicholls (1976) found that high achievers have a tendency to maintaining a high sense of competence. These studies reveal that n Ach is related to self-esteem. In order to find out the nature of relationship between n Ach and self-esteem in the present situation, an additional hypothesis, in this regard has been formulated and tested.

3. Achievement Motivation Vs Sex

Sharma (1972) studied achievement abasement need. Murray's n Ach and n Abs was in the study among 419 (225 male; 194 female) university students. The result indicated that females have higher achievement motivation than males.

Asghar Ali (1989) studied the n Ach of destitute boys and girls. The study was carried out for a sample of 100 subjects (49 boys and 51 girls)of 14 to 18 years age. The result indicated that, destitute girls are more motivated towards n Ach than that of boys. Kureshi Afzal (1979) studied the TAT motives of Hindu and Muslim adolescents for a sample of 199 adolescents. He found that n Ach was stronger in females than males.

Gokulnathan (1975) studied sex difference in the level of n Ach among secondary school students of two upper Assam plains. The result indicated that girls have more n Ach when compared to boys. Chaudhary Nirmala (1972) studied the relationship between n Ach and anxiety, intelligence, sex, social class and vocational aspiration among 200 boys and 229 girls studying higher secondary course. The result indicated that girls have higher n Ach as compared to boys. In a nationwide study of the consequences of the different home-backgrounds, Veroff, Atkinson, Feld and Gurin (1960) found different results for men and women, indicating women are lower in n Ach than men.

There is, in fact, evidence that women report lower estimates of their own abilities, performance and future prospects in some achievement situations even when they actually perform as well or better than men do. (Crandall, 1969; Meese Eccles *et. al.* 1982).

Thus, when some studies report that women have a higher n Ach than men, some others fail to confirm it. On the contrary, probably mediated by situational conditions, they report that women have lower n Ach than men.

Probably women did not respond to conditions designed to elicit this need the same way that men did (Mc Clelland, 1953), because there is evidence of a broad range of dispositional difference between the sexes (Deaux, 1975). Evidence of demographic behaviour is difficult to interpret because any presumed biologically based temperamental differences and socialisation pressure tend to act in the same direction.

Accordingly, Stein & Baily (1973) found that n Ach in women is related to different situations (such as social skills) than for men. This finding was supported by the results that n Ach in elementary school girls are directly related to girls' desire for approval and affiliation (Crandall, Katkovsky, and Preston, 1969) and that the n Ach scores have been unrelated to girls' social relation skills (Fadiman, 1960).

Additional supports have been found from the results that females fail to show an expected increase in n Ach scores when exposed to arousal conditions that stroll intelligence and leadership ability and that they do respond with increases in these scores when presented with arousal conditions involving social acceptance (Mc Clelland, *et.. al.* 1953).

This trend on sex difference in n Ach is viewed in two different ways, by two different psychologists.

(1) Horner (1972) viewed it as females' fear of success and striving to avoid it. But, subsequent researches on the fear of success have produced complex and inconsistent results with many studies failing to find sex difference (Tresemer, 1976, 1977; Zuckerman & Wheeler, 1975). Both conceptual and methodological issues remain to be settled, before the fear of success its relation to achievement motivation and nature of sex difference in each can be understood (Hyland *et. al.* 1985).

(2) A different root was led by Weiner (1972) to explain this phenomenon. He argued that achievement striving may be a more complex phenomenon among women than among men, because achievement behaviour in women conflicts with traditional female role. It is known from the studies conducted in US (Sears, Maccoby, & Levin, 1957) and cross cultural studies (Bary, Becon & Child, 1957) that boys generally receive more training and encouragement for achievement than girls.

While the results on difference in n Ach are

inconsistent, Hyland, Curtis and Mason (1985) argued that the relation between n Ach and behaviour measures on n Ach is lower in women than in men, and women do not show an increase in achievement imagery under achievement arousing conditions.

Studies conducted during the past two decades, on various populations reveal a contradiction on sex difference with regard to n Ach. Despite these discrepancies now-a-days females are given more opportunities and encouragement in education, occupation etc. So in order to identify the present trend on sex difference with respect to n Ach, gender has been included as a variable in the present study.

4. Achievement Motivation Vs Birth Order

De and Priya shampoo (1972) studied some personal and academic correlates of n Ach. 140 male students (50 from arts; 50 from science and 40 from commerce faculties) pursuing post graduate studies were selected for the study. The result indicated that difference between first borns and last borns were significant at 0.05 level. More precisely, first borns are high achievers than last borns. Fatmi (1990) found that there was no significant difference between subjects of different ordinal positions with regard to their n Ach except for first order and last order.

First born persons may also possess a relatively high need for achievement (Sampson, 1962) and a strong need for affiliation generally (Dember, 1964) although they are often comparatively unpopular in their social groups (Schachter, 1964a).

Rosen (1961) found that first born children have a higher need to achieve than later borns. This need to achieve may be an outcome of special relationship between first borns children and their parents. First borns have their parents' exclusive attention and seem to interact more with parents than other children (Gewirds & Gewirtz, 1965). Parents of first born also seem to expect more of them (Hilton, 1967). As a result, first borns may seek approval by conforming to adult standard including standard of achievement.

Though there is consistency in these results, in order to understand the trend in the present situation an additional hypothesis in this regard has been included and tested in the present study.

2. Self-esteem

1. Self-esteem – Characteristics

Self-esteem is related to so many aspects of life that it is difficult to make generalisations about cause and effect, though some evidence is suggestive. Social class, religion, ethnic group and traumatic experiences in childhood are only weakly related to self-esteem (Coopersmith, 1978).

One of the most important factors is the amount of parental attention and acceptance experienced in growing ups. High-esteem individuals tend to come from homes in which the parents have expressed a great deal of acceptance and relied on democratic methods of child rearing. Low- esteem individuals usually have been exposed to parental criticism and rejection, as well as to coercive methods of discipline (Graybill, 1978).

Garg (1981) studied the relationship between self-esteem and academic achievement. 300 students of XI std. in 15-17 years age group were selected for the study. It was found that self-esteem of upper caste students was found significantly greater than that of other caste students.

Waite Barbara (1990) reported a significant relationship between self-esteem and perceived competence. Cairns (1990) examined the stability of various aspects of self-concept advocated by Harter (1983) including Locus of control during late adolescence. Result showed the evidence of relative stability, especially among those whose environment had remained stable, while the trend was for modest positive increases in almost all aspects of self-esteem over the time period examined.

Adenekan Oyefeso and Pius A. Baiyere,(1990) studied the influence of self-esteem on affiliativeness among Nigerian adolescents. The study was carried out for a sample of 151 Nigerian adolescents (mean age of 17 years). Self-esteem was measured by Adanijo and Oyefeso's (1986) self – esteem scale and n Affiliation was measured by Edward's (1953) personal preference Schedule. The result indicated that adolescents with high self-esteem are more affiliative than those with low self esteem.

Burnett *et. al.* (1989) reported that decision making self-esteem, a typical component of self-esteem, correlated positively with independence of course choice, course satisfaction, course planning, career planning and career options.

These results indicate an important influence of self – esteem on decision making process. To find out the type of relationship an additional hypothesis in this regard has been tested in the present study.

2. Self-esteem Vs Sex

Karim Shamin (1990) reported that sex difference, appeared to have profound effects on the personally perceived self and socially perceived self. Monterio (1978) found that women generally had lower self-esteem than men. Cairns (1990) reported that gender difference, favouring males were also common.

Other lines of evidence, however, do provide some support for the original conclusion. By high school age, females are more oriented toward externality on the IE Scale indicating that they perceive themselves to be less able to control major events in their lives (Samuel, 1980). Females also appeared to have a lower opinion of their own abilities as indicated by a preference for games of luck over those of skill- the opposite of the preference expressed by most males (Deaux *et. al.* 1975). Assuming there is a genuine sex difference in self–esteem, it could contribute to the sex difference in conformity that was mentioned earlier.

Several investigations have compared males and females on various components of self-esteem, and the general finding has been that females tend to score lower (Janis & Field 1959). Maccoby and Jacklin (1974) disputed this assessment on the grounds that more recent research has not found such a sex difference.

Garg (1981) found that sex factor did not affect significantly the self-esteem scores of adolescents, indicating that there is no sex difference with regard to self-esteem. Tashakkori (1990) found that self beliefs and the related proximal psychological variables seem to be better predicators of self-esteem and its change than are distal socio demographic variables.

Hall Evelyn (1990) reported that initial performance expectancies were significantly correlated with skill level indicating that performance expectancies may be more related to skill than gender. Data do not support Corbin's (1990) finding that females express less confidence than males for future performance.

While the studies on self-esteem with regard to

sex reveal inconsistent results Cheryl Ormond *et. al.*, (1991) found that males scored higher than females on decision self-esteem. In order to confirm this aspect, an additional hypothesis is included in the present study and tested.

3. Self-esteem Vs Birth order

Bolaji K.Yusuff (1990) studied a comparative analysis of birth order and self-esteem among university athletes. The sample was 104 university students (64 male and 40 female). The result showed that with the exception of first born and second born females, there is a significant difference between Birth Order and self-esteem. This result implies that first born males have higher self-esteem than later borns. But this difference was not significant with regard to females.

These results seem to be not clear. Why is there a significant difference in different Birth orders with respect to self-esteem among males and not among females? Whether this same finding holds good for the typical component of Decision making self-esteem also? are some of the aspects that need to be studied. In order to bridge this gap, an additional hypothesis is tested in the present study.

STUDIES IN SPECIFIC

Studies conducted on decision making styles, decision making process and its correlates relevant to the present study have been reviewed under this heading.

DECISION MAKING STYLES

1. Decision Making Styles – Characteristics

Based on the level of conflict, Janis and Mann (1977)

described five behaviour patterns that individuals used to cope with stressful decisional situations, viz. Unconflicted adherence, unconflicted change, Defensive avoidance, Hyper vigilance and Vigilance. It was validated by Burnett *et. al.* (1989).

According to Tallman, *et. al.* (1990) a choice is a microcosm of the social and behavioural forces affecting a given action at the individual and collective levels. Fredrickson's (1986) findings indicate that variation in motives and performance affect the decision making process. Feather & Mann (1982) found that masculinity was positively correlated with non-vigilant styles. Bond (1981) reported that External Locus of control was positively correlated with Defensive avoidance and Hypervigilance.

Lunneborg (1978) related decision making styles, as assessed by Harren's (1976) Assessment of career Decision Making, to measures whether a major had been chosen, certainty about the major, satisfaction with occupation. The planning decision making styles, which is similar to the vigilant style, was positively correlated with certainty and satisfaction with career choice. The dependent style, which is similar to defensive avoidance, was negatively correlated with career certainty and satisfaction.

Berger-Cross, Kahn, and Weare (1983) tested the relationship between Harren's (1976) decision making styles and measures of satisfaction at University, involvement with peers and teaching staff, and occupational commitment. The planning style was positively correlated with satisfaction, involvement with peers and staff, and occupational commitment. The dependent style was negatively correlated with satisfaction at university, involvement with teaching staff and occupational commitment.

Burnett *et. al.* (1989), in the validation study of Flinders Decision making Questionnaire on course decision making by students, found that independence of course choice, satisfaction with course and course planning correlated positively with vigilant decision making style and negatively with non-vigilant styles. But with an exception, on the contrary to prediction, Hyper vigilance and career planning were not related.

Cheryl Ormond *et. al.* (1991) studied metacognitive analysis of decision making in adolescence using Flinders Adolescence Decision making Questionnaire. The result showed that metacognitive knowledge related significantly with vigilant and maladaptive decision making styles and decision self –esteem. This result indicates that metacognitive knowledge (person, task and strategy) is a significant predicator of performance in the domain of decision making.

Svenson *et. al.* (1990) studied the effects of time pressure on choice and judgment. Contrary to expectation, it was found that common attribute information was used less and that there was no increased importance of negative information under time pressure. Instead, time pressure resulted in a shift toward greater preference for the subjects with the highest school grades. Plante Thomas et al (1990) reported that defensive coping style (as measured by lie scale of EPQ) is associated with the amount of time spent in leisure activities.

Kozelsski's (1981) findings provide an insight in the role of the environment and the personality determinants of risky decision, such as the trait of decision maker, the achievement motive, the need for aggression and dominance.

These studies reveal an overview about the correlates of decision making process and in particular, the important influence of personality on decision making process. The following studies also confirm this fact.

2. Personlity Dimensions Vs Decision Making

Richter and Tosvold (1980) reported that personality factors like high ego-strength, imaginativeness, dominant personality, initiative, self-sufficiency or independence in thought, intelligence etc., show their impact on decisions made by a decision maker. Thanick and Vendel (1983) found that personality traits do have some relationship with decision making. They found that the undecided pupils have greater dependence on personality traits like submissiveness and lack of initiation. In the same line Rokeach and Barron (1960, 1963) also found that the strong ego-strength and independence in thought are related to creative solution of the problem by the individual. Moore *et. al.* (1990) studied decision making process of youth. Result showed that there was a significant negative correlation between levels of anxiety and commitment to previous chosen course of action.

Davis Donald *et. al.* (1990) studied the experimental application of personality type as an analogue for decision making style. 96 Graduate students were classified in 1 of 4 decision making [DM] styles according to the Myers-Briggs Type indicator [MBTI]. These were sensing thinking, sensing feeling, intuiting thinking and intuiting feeling styles. Subjects then performed 13 DM tasks in an interacting computer-stimulated business environment and their cost performance [CP] was measured. There was a significant difference in CP among the 4 DM styles. Overall, sensing types performed most efficient than intuition types. Personality as determined by the MBTI appears to be promising as an analog for DM style in an operational Decision environment.

Priyamvada Srivastava (1989) studied the relationship between decision making ability and 16 factors of personality. The result showed that among 16 factors, factor I (Tender-minded –Tough-minded) and M (Imaginative-Practical) showed significant relationship with decision making skills. Precisely the Tender minded and Imaginative manager showed better decision making than Tough minded and Practical managers.

The growth of knowledge about competent decision making is mediated by a host of social and personality factors including experiences in family and peer decisions and a strengthening of self confidence (Keating, 1990).

These studies show that the personality of the decision maker highly influences the decision making process (Hunt Raymond *et. al.*, 1989), skills and abilities. As such, for the past 10 years. In a deeper sense, psychologists have been attempting to study the relationship between the specific personality dimensions and the specific decision making styles.

For example, Campbell (1981) found that Neuroticism was positively correlated with Defensive avoidance and Hyper vigilance. Beswick (1981) found that anxiety and assertiveness are related to Janis and Mann decision making styles. Feather and Mann,(1982) found that depression is related to Janis and Mann decision making styles. Olof (1990) found that impulsiveness (Neuroticism) is negatively correlated with the tendency to rationalize. Bolger Nial (1990) reported that Neuroticism influences coping effort and increases in daily anxiety under stress.

Meena Sehgal (1984) studied the effect of Psychoticism and reinforcement of vigilance. The study was carried out for the population of university girls. Psychoticism was measured by EPQ(R) and the vigilance was measured through a visual vigilance task involving signal detection. The result indicated that the subjects low on Psychoticism were superior in vigilance. Radford et.al. (1986) found that depression in psychiatric patients was related to Janis and Mann's (1977) decision making styles. They found that severity of psychiatric disturbances (as assessed by General psychoneurotic disorder and depression) was positively correlated with Defensive avoidance.

These studies seem to support the notion that personality dimensions are important correlates of decision making styles. In order to confirm the results the present study has been attempted.

3. Achievement Motivation Vs Decision Making Styles

Slade *et. al.* (1991) found that positively motivated subjects shifted faster than negatively motivated subjects to more difficult tasks over time, indicating high achievers are more vigilant and risk taking.

Rim (1963) conducted a study with Israeli University students. It was found that subjects scoring high on index of achievement motivation tend to take more risks in their initial decision than low scoring subjects.

Mahone (1960) found, among male college students, that students who were low in achievement motivation and high in achievement anxiety (Ms<Mf) were more likely to be unrealistic (in their decision) than the students with the opposite pattern of motivation and anxiety. The Atkinson model has also received support

(for men but not for women) from a study of curricular choices of college students (Isaacson, 1964).

Zamft Hyman, (1975) found that students belonging to decision making group had a greater need for higher order needs of achievement, autonomy and dominance than did students belonging to social group and non-involved group.

Since the decision conflict model is of recent origin there is no adequate investigation to show the relationship between the decision coping pattern and achievement motivation. In order to fill in this gap, an attempt has been made in the present study in that direction.

4. Self-esteem Vs Decision Making Styles

Govind Tiwari (1983) studied the relationship between self-esteem and risky decisions. The study was carried out for a sample of 700 adolescent girls (age 14-17 years). Self-esteem was measured by Thakur's Self-esteem Inventory. The result showed that positive self-esteem promotes risky decision whereas moderate and negative self-esteem demotes. Rardford (1982), Distefano, Pryor and Smith (1997) and Mann *et. al.* (1989) found that a good decision maker tends to have a high level of self esteem and confidence in his or her own ability.

Feather and Mann (1982) found that self-esteem is related to Janis and Mann's (1977) decision making styles. Paul c. Burnett *et. al.*'s (1991) findings empirically validated Janis and Mann's (1977) link between decision making self-esteem and decision styles. In order to confirm the result in Indian setting, Decision making self-esteem has been included in the present study.

5. Sex and Birth order Vs Decision Making Styles

As there are very few studies to our knowledge, to explain the relationship between some of the demographic variables like sex and Birth order and Decision Making Styles, attempts have been made in the present study to find out the influence of demographic variables on Decision Making Styles.

SUMMARY

The multiplicity of studies referred to in this chapter reveal that among the correlates of decision making styles, personality seems to be an important one. But, as the decision conflict model is of recent origin, very few studies have been carried out using personality dimensions to explain the decision making styles, especially using Extraversion. That is, there is no adequate investigation to definitely prove the relationship between the decision coping pattern (as proposed by conflict model) and the personality dimensions and demographic variables.

So, the knowledge of relationship between personality dimensions and decision making styles is a gap in our knowledge. As the knowledge of the relationship between personality dimensions and decision making styles has implication for Guidance and counseling situation, attempt has been made to study the decision making styles in relation to some personality characteristics of university students.

3

Theoretical Perspective of Decision Making Theories

THEORETICAL PERSPECTIVE OF DECISION MAKING PROCESS AND THEORIES

The decision-making theory has long been recogniSed as an area of interest in the Social Science and traditionally researches have been conducted on the quantitative aspects of decision making and decision process (Edwards and Tversky, 1967; Miller and Starr 1967).

Decision theory aims to predict choice on the basis of individual's beliefs about the probabilities of various outcomes of each of the alternatives he / she considers open to him/her and his/her evaluation of those outcomes (Vroom, 1964). Fishbein & Ajzen (1975) termed the sum of the products of these two variables (beliefs and evaluation) as 'the attitude towards that alternative'.

According to Atkins (1988) decision making process can be characterised by three kinds of alternatives: analysis, synthesis and evaluation. Essentially this is a cognitive process. Cheryl Ormond's (1991) findings lend support to the assumption that knowledge about cognitive process is a co-requisite for competent decision-making.

Newell and Simon (1972) Flavel and Wellman (1977) identified three categories of metacognitive knowledge, which have guided the research on metacognition. Firstly, person knowledge pertains to knowledge of inter and intra-individual differences in traits, characteristics and limitation in performing a cognitive activity. Second, task knowledge relates to understanding how characteristics of cognitive activity may affect performance. Third, strategy knowledge refers to knowledge about techniques or procedures involved in cognitive activities and their regulations.

The main concern here is the strategy knowledge that manifests with a decisional outcome. A strategy is one of the outcome dimensions of dependent variables of the decision making process and a media through which we can view the decision making process. Based on the decision outcome manifested, strategy knowledge can be identified. In this identification process the decision making process, an abstract phenomenon, is converted into concrete, an observable and recordable phenomenon.

Hence possibly with precision, decision making processes are studied empirically, through strategies. Psychologists have long back attempted to assign strategy dimension to the decision making process and analysed human behaviour pattern. The following are some of the classifications of strategies adopted by psychologists. These classifications are based on different aspects of decision making processes to identify the decision making style of an individual.

(a) Decision making strategies identified by Dinklage

Dinklage (1966) identified eight strategies, as adopted by High school students.

1.**Impulsive:** taking the first alternative with little thought or examination. The individual does not look before he leaps. Due to time pressure or inborn characteristic of impulsivity the individual frequently follows this strategy and takes a decision all of a sudden.

2. **Compliant**: Letting someone else to decide. In order to avoid taking a decision or the risk, the individual shifts the responsibility of taking a decision to some other persons and the individual abides whatever the other people say.

3. **Fatalistic**: Leaving it up to the environment or fate. Being pessimistic and low level of self-confidence the individual feels that it's all in the cards. He takes any form of decision. It may be an impulsive decision or a compliant decision.

4. **Delaying**: Postponing thought and action. For want of sufficient information or fear of the consequences, the individual decides to cross the bridge later. There is none to shift the responsibility to and hence the individual delays taking a decision with an expectation that any external assistance would help him in course of time.

5. **Agonising:** Becoming overwhelmed in analysing alternatives. Being in an aggressive mood and emotionality, the individual does not know what to do. Due to time pressure or such external forces, in order to cope with the situation, the individual takes overwhelming decisions without any reasoning.

6. Planning: Using a rational procedure with balance between reason and emotion. In this strategy, the individual carefully analyses the situation and weighs the facts of the future outcome and takes a decision suitable to the problem at hand.

7. Intuitive: Taking a decision based on inner harmony. In this strategy, the individual is not in a stirred up emotional state or time pressure. He does not take a decision with careful analysis but takes the decision that comes to his mind that he feels right at that moment.

8. Paralysis: Accepting responsibility but unable to approach a decision. In this strategy the individual is in a decision dilemma for a long time not knowing how to face it. He is able to neither avoid the problem nor approach it.

An analysis of these strategies reveals that even though there are eight strategies, some of them seem to overlap. For example, Fatalistic decision overlaps with Impulsive and Compliant decision. Paralysis decision overlaps with delaying decisions. Some strategies like intution and agonising are implicit entities. Thus, even though this approach identifies, classifies, and studies different decision coping patterns, these patterns lack in primary (principal) dimensions and empirical views.

(b) Decision making Strategies identified by Gelatt, Varenhorst and Richard Carey

Gelatt, Varenhorst and Richard Carey (1973) have classified decision making strategies into four on the basis of element of risk involved.

1. The wish strategy: It involves alternatives that could lead to the most desirable result regardless of risk. Fulfilling the wish is the only criterion adopted in this strategy. As the other aspects like the probability of success are neglected, this would not be a good decision unless a chance occurs.

2. The escape strategy: It involves choosing the alternative that is most likely to avoid the worst possible result. In embarrassing situations, individuals try to escape from the decision and as a result they try to avoid. When the individual is pessimistic he believes that the decision will not give a fruitful result. So the individual tries to minimise the loss and hence escapes from the decision situation.

3. The safe strategy: It involves choosing the alternative that is most likely to bring success. In this strategy, the individual considers only the probability of occurrence of a particular alternative. The satisfaction of values or the fulfillment of wishes is not considered here. The individual selects an alternative that has a high probability of success.

4. The combination strategy: It involves choosing the alternative that combines high probability and high desirability. In this strategy the individual adopts both the wish criterion and safety criterion. When the individual expects a gain or he optimistically approaches a problem he adopts the combination strategy.

(c) Decision making strategies identified by Kogan and Wallach

Based on the risks involved in making a decision, Kogan and Wallach (1967) identified two types of decision strategies.

1. Risk taking decision: Risk taking decision involves taking hard decision and facing the challenging situation courageously. Risk taking is based on two important inherent aspects: lack of certainty and prospect of loss (or failure) resulting from the decision. Kogan and Wallach (1967) pointed out that to talk about 'risk taking' is to refer to behaviours in situations where there is a desirable goal but lack of certainty that it can be attained. However, an individual is willing to take such a risky decision, considering the chance outcome (or skill outcomes), the type and the extent of information available to him/her, the gain or cost, real incentives, the previous success or failures etc.

2. Risk avoiding decisions: Risk avoiding decisions styles involves escaping from making decision. Persons who are externals (chance outcomes), not willing to gather information about the problem (less information available to the decision maker), pessimistic and anxious (greater perceived cost—Wine, 1971) and have experienced frequent failures and have low level of self-esteem, with one or more of these characteristics, tend to take a risk avoiding decision.

According to this approach, individual adopt a decision style suitable to the situation. A decision strategy adopted without considering the situation will lead to maladjustment. In this approach, the decision strategies are analysed in terms of the situation and hence provide a complete knowledge about decision making process.

(d) Decision making Strategies identified by Tversky and Kahneman

Tversky and Kahneman (1974) believed that people simplify their decisions by using heuristics. They described the heuristic decision making rules of Representations, Availability and Adjustment.

1. Representativeness: In judging on the basis of representativeness, people decide whether the situation fits or is part of another situation. That is if a problem looks like another problem, the decision taken for the former one also suits to the present problem. The more nearly the problem is representative, the more suitable the solution to the present situation. The individual matches the problem one to one and makes a judgement which best fits the situation.

Judgment on the basis of representativeness, however, is likely to lead to errors. First, the frequency of success of the first problem is ignored. Unless one has prior knowledge, the individual cannot be successful in this strategy. Second, in judging the probabilities of outcome for Representativeness, people tend to overlook the effect that the size of the sample will have on the estimate made of the likelihood of an event. Third, in making the decision on the basis of Representativeness, the individual may also be a victim of the gamblers fallacy. To some extent these errors can be reduced with good memory. This leads to another judgment heuristic known as Availability.

(2) Availability: Some events are easier to remember than others. Because frequent events are generally easier to remember than infrequent ones, the case with which we remember certain things help us in making subjective probability estimates. In other words, easily remembered events are actually likely to be more frequent than others. Estimating subjective probability, in this way can be useful. But by neglecting events that are harder to remember, this heuristic can obviously lead to misjudgment about the likelihood of certain outcomes. On such occasions, individuals escape using two sorts of adjustments that follow.

(3) Adjustments: The subjective probability estimates are sometimes arrived at by using the heuristic known as adjustment. The individuals start with certain subjective probability and adjust and raise or lower it depending on the circumstances. When adjustments are made, the outcome is much dependent upon the starting point. If one starts with a high estimate and adjusts it downward his probability estimate will be higher than what it will be when he starts with a lower estimate. It is the initial level provided that biases the estimates. This biasing effect is known as anchoring. Even then, this adjustment is only a rough estimation and fairly undergoes changes from situation to situation and individual to individual.

(e) Decision making strategies suggested by James *et. al.*

James *et. al.* (1972) suggest the following decision making strategies applied in counseling situations.

(1) Authoritarian model: This model involves the individuals choosing the alternative which the authoritarian suggests. Whatever the authorities like parents, teachers, or elders suggest, the individual strictly adopts it. So the resultant decision is fairly predictable.

(2) Laissez Faire model : This model involves the individual's efforts in sorting out the important factors and to move in reasonable ways independently with very little information from outside. The individual deciding at his own discretion is the important aspect of this model.

(3) Maximum gain model: This model is most effected by the possible personal gain that will accrue to the individual, ignoring several meaningful factors while concentrating on gain. For example, probability of occurrence, or the person's own abilities are not considered.

(4) Mathematical model: This model involves choosing a decision in the light of probabilities, and costs and benefits. Here the individual safeguards himself by considering the probability of occurrences of his decision along with the gain.

(5) Trait and factor model: This model involves, matching the traits with the choice requirements or factors, with some compromise. This is the earnest model of vocational choice espoused by Parsons. This model describes a generally static process in which neither the individual nor the choice can change.

(6) Stochastic model: The concept of Stochastic model presumes that following a decision where there are two independent paths to be followed. A decision to follow one course denies the facts or probability of the other (stochastic = one way). This is nearly similar to approach and avoidance conflict situation.

(7) Gelatt's sequential model: This model involves defining the objective, collecting the data, studying the possible alternatives and evaluating them before making a decision. As the name implies Gelatt (1962) proposed this model.

(f) Decision making strategy identified by Harren

On the assessment of career decision making process Harren (1976) identified two types of decision making styles.

(1) Planning decision making: Individuals spend some time on planning with various occupational choices and the future scopes in light of their own abilities, personal values, probabilities of success etc. In this style, the individuals themselves involve in vigorous information processing and select their own choices.

According to Subjective Expected Utility (SEU) theorists, in planning decision making, individuals choose one action among a possible set of actions on the basis of their values (perceived costs and benefits) of the possible outcomes of each action. The SEU corresponding to particular action is the weighed sum of the values attached to that action's possible outcomes where the weights are the perceived probability of each outcome. A rational decision maker takes the action with the highest SEU value relative to alternative actions (Von Winterfeldt and Edwards, 1986).

(2) Dependent decision making: On the other hand, some individuals for fear of solution to a good choice or for want of sufficient information, they depend on their parents or elders or their own friends in selecting their future career. In a dependent style of decision making, the individual is fully dependent on others. At times, when the other person does not know the ability and difficulty of the individual, there is no use of a decision.

In planning decision-making the individual makes his own choices. So it would be a better decision-making method than a dependent decision making method.

The decision-making strategies so far mentioned are based on the subjective entities like subjective values, subjective probabilities, loss and gain, etc. Even though we acknowledge that it is the importance we give to components of decision making which influences perception of situations and problem and which results in decision, their significance to the individuals of affective components of their process have been neglected by the researchers (Gordon, 1975). Because Mac Crimmon (1973), defined decision making as the process of thought and action not of affect that culminates in choice behaviour.

Further, they fail to study the decisional outcome based on situational determinants. Because decision-making is primarily focused on choosing one course of action from a possibly many. The choice is made within a context and is influenced by elements of the environment. Decision makers, therefore, are bombarded by environmental restraints such as available time and resources (as well as the personal constraints of skill, knowledge and processing capacity).

More recently psychologists lay emphasis on the stimulus or situational conditions to study the decision behavior empirically. These attempts provided a more general view of decision-making process covering all the decision-making styles mentioned earlier. One such attempt was carried out by Janis and Mann, who studied the decision-making styles in conflicting situations.

(g) Decision making strategies identified by Janis and Mann

Despite the diversities of decision-making strategies mentioned, based on a thorough search of research literature, recently a more comprehensive classification of strategies was adopted by Janis and Mann (1977). They studied decisional outcome (response) on the basis of conflict (stimulus) situations.

As the individuals tend to exhibit their predominant (true colour) decision making strategy only at the time of conflicts, this model is capable of identifying the underlying characteristics of individuals during decision making process. In this sense this model is a better predictor of human decision pattern.

On analysing the decisional outcome, based on conflicts involved, they identified five decision strategies viz.

(i) Unconflicted adherence

(ii) Unconflicted change

(iii) Defensive avoidance

(iv) Hyper vigilance

(v) Vigilance

1. Unconflicted adherence: When there is no need for a change in whatever the course of action that one does, the individual complacently decides to continue it, ignoring the information about risk of losses. Here conflict does not arise and the individual adherence to what he does. This strategy is unconflicted adherenc. But all through the life, one cannot mind only one action/course of action. So, sometimes as the time passes by one has to change the course of action and switch over to another course of action.

2. Unconflicted change: When the individual wants to change the course of action, he simply passes over to the next action that he wanted to attend to. Here, there is only one course of action to be attended to and hence, the problem of conflict does not arise. Though there is no conflict the course of action is changed only for a change. The individual uncritically adopts whichever new course of action is most salient.

In these two styles, there is no conflict, only one alternative i.e. either the one he does or the one he has to attend to is predominant. But the personal values and the social forces that act upon it are not so simple for an individual to change his course of action simply and uncritically. When the individual wants to change his course of action, more than one alternative having nearly equal forces arise. As a result, the individual has to face a conflicting situation.

3. **Defensive avoidance**: When the individual perceives conflict, he is in a position to select one he alternative to execute. Sometimes the conflict is tremendously difficult and embarrassing. In this situation, in order to defend the ego and fear of meeting the consequence, the individual tries to escape from the situation by avoiding to take a decision. This is Defensive avoidance.

Janis and Mann found that this kind of defensive avoidance takes place in three forms viz. (a) Procrastination, (b) Buck passing and (c) Rationalisation. If the individual avoids taking a decision by withholding or putting off the decisions, it is Procratination. If the individual avoids taking decisions by shifting the responsibility of taking a decision to some other individual it is Buck Passing. If the individual avoids the reality of decisions by giving reasons thereof, it is Rationalisation.

Both in Procrastination and in Buck passing, the individual does not take a decision of his own. In procrastination the individual decides not to decide and in Buck passing the individual decides to take a decision with the help of others. But in Rationalisation, the individual takes a decision of any kind but rationalises it when it goes wrong. In general, all three avoidance coping styles do not give a fruitful effect but lead to maladaptive behaviour pattern.

4. **Hyper vigilance**: When the individuals are

confident enough to make a decision, they do not avoid taking a decision but face the situation. If there is no sufficient time to analyze the problem, the individual is helpless and takes hyper-vigilant decisions. Here the individuals perceive that time pressure to be predominant. For a way out of dilemma they frantically seize up on hastily contrived solutions that seem to promise immediate relief.

5. Vigilance: In the vigilance strategy, the individual perceives a conflict and time pressure but they neither avoid nor take a decision that seize upon a hastily contrived solution. But with a confidence, the individual patiently classifies, analyses, organizes and synthesizes, compares and integrates various aspects of the alternatives together with the pros and cons of each alternative and selects the one which best satisfies his values and objectives. Thus, vigilance involves a 'high quality of information processing' (Cheryl Ormond *et. al.*, 1991).

The extent to which an individual is vigilant and arrives at the most appropriate solution depends upon how large information the individual processes at a time (range or span of thought or information) and in one aspect and that what relevant factors (variables) does he include in the information processing and finding out the contributing factors that suit to his present problem or objective.

SUMMARY

The relationship between vigilant information processing as postulated by Janis and Mann (1977) and decision outcomes has been tested for decision makers in international crisis (Herek, *et. al.* 1987). The model has also formed the basis for successful attempts to improve the quality of decision making in adults (Mann *et. al.,* 1989) and adolescents (Mann *et. al.,* 1988).

As life is becoming more and more unpredictable, the chances for having to make decisions in conflicting situations are more. Identifying the decision making styles of individuals in such a conflicting situation can aid in helping people who make a defective decision and the characteristics that promote such decision styles. Hence the decision making styles postulated by Janis and Mann is more appropriate among the different decision making theories.

4

Plan and Procedure

OBJECTIVES OF THE PRESENT STUDY

The present study attempts to investigate the decision making styles of university students in relation to decision making self esteem, personality dimensions (extraversion, neuroticism, and psychoticism) and achievement motivation. The objective of the study are as follow.

The major objectives of this study are:

1. To find out the relationship between self esteem as decision maker and decision making styles.
2. To find out the relationship between personality dimensions and decision making styles.
3. To find out the relationship between achievement motivation and decision making styles.
4. To find oust the relationship between personality dimensions and self-esteem as decision maker.
5. To find out the relationship between self esteem as decision maker and achievement motivation.
6. To find out the relationship between personality dimensions and achievement motivation.

The minor objectives of this study are:

1. To find out the decision making self-esteem of males and females.
2. To find out the decision making styles of males and females.
3. To find out the personality characteristics of males and females.
4. To find out the difference in achievement motivation between males and females.
5. To find out the decision making self-esteem of professional course students and non-professional course students.
6. To find out the decision making styles of professional course students and non-professional course students.
7. To find out the personality characteristics of professional course students and non-professional course students.
8. To find out the difference in achievement motivation between professional course students and non-professional course students.
9. To find out the decision making self-esteem of students of different order of birth.
10. To find out the decision making styles of students of different orders of birth.
11. To find out the personality dimensions of students of different orders of birth.
12. To find out the differences in achievement motivation of students of different orders of birth.

STATEMENT OF HYPOTHESES

A review of related studies show that the results are not satisfactory due to contradictory findings. The present investigation was planned taking into consideration such contradictions. Accordingly the following hypotheses were formulated.

Major Hypotheses

1. THERE IS A SIGNIFICANT RELATIONSHIP BETWEEN SELF-ESTEEM AS A DECISION MAKER AND DECISION MAKING STYLES.

1-1 There is a significant positive relationship between self-esteem as a decision maker and vigilant decision making style.

1-2 There is a significant negative relationship between self-esteem as a decision maker and hyper vigilant decision making style.

1-3 There is a significant negative relationship between self-esteem as a decision maker and Defensive avoidance decision making style.

1-4 There is a significant negative relationship between self-esteem as a decision maker and Procrastination decision making style.

1-5 There is a significant negative relationship between self-esteem as a decision maker and Buck passing decision making style.

1-6 There is a significant negative relationship between self-esteem as a decision maker and Rationalisation decision making style.

2. THERE IS A SIGNIFICANT RELATIONSHIP BETWEEN PERSONALITY DIMENSIONS AND DECISION MAKING STYLES.

2-1.1 There is a significant positive relationship

between Extraversion and vigilant decision making style.

2-1.2 There is a significant negative relationship between Extraversion and hyper vigilant decision making style

2-1.3 There is a significant negative relationship between Extraversion and Defensive avoidance decision making style.

2-1.4 There is a significant negative relationship between Extraversion and Procrastination decision making style.

2-1.5 There is a significant negative relationship between Extraversion and Buck passing decision making style.

2-1.6 There is a significant negative relationship between Extraversion and Rationalisation decision making style

2-2.1 There is a significant negative relationship between Neuroticism and vigilant decision making style.

2-2.2 There is a significant positive relationship between neuroticism and hyper vigilant decision making style

2-2.3 There is a significant positive relationship between neuroticism and Defensive avoidance decision making style.

2-2.4 There is a significant positive relationship between neuroticism and Procrastination decision making style.

2-2.5 There is a significant positive relationship between neuroticism and Buck passing decision making style.

2-2.6 There is a significant positive relationship between neuroticism and Rationalisation decision making style

2-3.1 There is a significant negative relationship between psychoticism and vigilant decision making style.

2-3.2 There is a significant positive relationship between psychoticism and hyper vigilant decision making style

2-3.3 There is a significant positive relationship between psychoticism and Defensive avoidance decision making style.

2-3.4 There is a significant positive relationship between psychoticism and Procrastination decision making style.

2-3.5 There is a significant positive relationship between psychoticism and Buck passing decision making style.

2-3.6 There is a significant positive relationship between psychoticism and Rationalisation decision making style

3. THERE IS A SIGNIFICANT RELATIONSHIP BETWEEN N ACH AND DECISION MAKING STYLES.

3-1 There is a significant positive relationship between n Ach and vigilant decision making style

3-2 There is a significant negative relationship between n Ach and hyper vigilant decision making style

3-3 There is a significant negative relationship between n Ach and Defensive avoidance decision making style.

3-4 There is a significant negative relationship between n Ach and Procrastination decision making style.

3-5 There is a significant negative relationship between n Ach and Buck passing decision making style.

3-6 There is a significant negative relationship between n Ach and Rationalisation decision making style

4. THERE IS A SIGNIFICANT RELATIONSHIP BETWEEN PERSONALITY DIMENSIONS AND SELF-ESTEEM AS A DECISION MAKER.

4.1 There is a significant positive relationship between Extraversion and self esteem decision maker.

4.2 There is a significant negative relationship between Neuroticism and Self-esteem as a decision maker.

4.3 There is a significant negative relationship between Psychoticism and self-esteem as a decision maker.

5. THERE IS A SIGNIFICANT POSITIVE RELATIONSHIP BETWEEN N ACH AND SELF-ESTEEM AS A DECISION MAKER

6. THERE IS SIGNIFICANT RELATIONSHIP BETWEEN PERSONALITY DIMENSIONS AND N ACH.

6.1 There is a significant positive relationship between Extraversion n Ach.

6.2 There is a significant negative relationship between Neuroticism n Ach.

6.3 There is a significant negative relationship between Psychoticism n Ach.

Sub - Hypotheses

1. There is no significant difference between males and females with regard to Self-esteem as a decision maker.
2. There is no significant difference between males and females with regard to decision-making styles.
3. There is no significant difference between males and females with regard to personality dimensions.
4. There is no significant difference between males and females with regard to n Ach.
5. There is no significant difference between professional course students and non-Professional course students with regard to Self-esteem and decision maker.
6. There is no significant difference between professional course students and non-Professional course students with regard to decision making styles.
7. There is no significant difference between professional course students and non-Professional course students with regard to personality dimensions.
8. There is no significant difference between professional course students and non-Professional course students with regard to n Ach.
9. There is no significant difference between students of different orders of birth with regard to self-esteem as a decision maker.
10. There is no significant difference between students of different orders of birth with regard to decision making styles.

11. There is no significant difference between students of different orders of birth with regard to personality dimensions.
12. There is no significant difference between students of different orders of birth with regard to n Ach.

SELECTION OF SAMPLE AND DESIGN

The population for this study is comprised of the students from various faculties of Annamalai University. The subjects have been drawn faculty-wise namely Engineering, Medicine, Dentistry, Agriculture, Education, Arts and Science.

A stratified random sampling technique was used to select the subjects. Final year students of different faculties were chosen for the present study. Printed questionnaires were distributed to 200 students selected randomly from various faculties, out of which 86 have to be rejected for want of reliable information, as the lie score was higher than the norm.

The sample consists of males (n=63) and females (n=51). On the basis of students studying in different courses, the sample was classified into two groups viz. Professional course students (n=67) and Non-professional course students (n=47). Based on the birth order of the students the sample was classified into three groups viz. First borns (n=51), Second borns (n=30) and Later borns (n=33).

In order to test the hypotheses, linear correlation statistical model was employed. A correlation matrix has been obtained for the scores of the psychological variables involved in the study. With the sub-groups two randomised group design and more than two randomised group design were employed. T tests and F tests have been computed to test the sub-hypotheses.

JUSTIFICATION OF THE SAMPLE

Early adolescence to middle adolescence is a crucial period in the development of decision making skills as it is for other cognitive domains (Keating, 1990). During early adolescence the ability to make competent decisions evolves, and by about the age of 15 years, most adolescents make decisions in ways similar to adults (Mann, Harmoni and Power, 1988).

The transition from childhood to adult thought during early to middle adolescents seems to bring a significant increase in competence on different cognitive process that facilitates tasks involved in sound decision making. Hence the subjects for the present investigation have been selected at early adulthood (with the mean age of 21.21 years) wherein the cognitive development or the development of decision making skills reach its optimum level.

According to the authors, the conflict model of decision making styles helps to find out the decision making styles in making personal decisions like career choice, marriage, health problems, etc. Now a days these are some of the major problems of the youngsters especially the problems of college students because, they have to make such choices in the near future. An understanding of the relationship between personality dimensions and decision making styles would help to provide them guidance and counseling. Therefore, the college students have been selected for the present study.

TOOLS

The data for the present study were collected with the help of the following tools (Questionnaires), which were originally validated by the authors. However, the reliability and validity were found out during the present investigation.

Questionnaire I : Eysenck Personality Questionnaire (EPQ – R)

Questionnaire II : Achievement Motivation Scale (AMS)

Questionnaire III : Flinders Decision Making Questionnaire I (DMQ – I)

Questionnaire IV : Flinders Decision Making Questionnaire II (DMQ – II)

DESCRIPTION OF TOOLS

Questionnaire I

EYSENCK PERSONALITY QUESTIONNAIRE – R

Eysenck Personality Questionnaire (Revised) – short version, was developed by Eysenck *et. al.* (1985). It was developed and standardised for adults.

This test measures the personality dimensions of individuals. The personality dimensions as measured by the EPQ – R are Extraversion (E), Neuroticism (N) and psychoticism (P). Three sub-scales of EPQ-R measure the extent of an individual's E, N and P dimension of personality. Eysenck H.J., the author of this test has included one more sub-scale called the lie scale to measure the extent to which the individual gives unreliable responses. So the lie scale provides a check on the reliability of the responses given by the individuals. In the present study, individuals who scored more than 7 (the mean of the lie score in the present sample) were not taken into account for want of reliable responses.

On the whole, the test EPQ-R consists of four sub-scales, namely Extraversion, Neuroticism, Psychoticism and Lie scale. Each scale consists of 12 items. So, the test on the whole consists of 48 items. Each item is followed by two alternative responses 'YES' and 'NO'. The individual is to respond by encircling the alternative as applicable to him/her. Score for each response is given according to the scoring procedure prepared by the author of the test.

Questionnaire II

ACHIEVEMENT MOTIVATION SCALE (AMS)

This scale was developed by Shah Beena (1986). This test measures the achievement motivation of an individual under four areas, viz.

1. Need for Academic Success.
2. Need for Vocational Achievement.
3. Need for Social Achievement and
4. Need for Skill Achievement.

Therefore, the scale consists of 4 sub-scales measuring achievement motivation under each area.

Each sub-scale consists of 10 items. The whole scale consists of 40 items. Each item is followed by 3 alternatives which the subjects have to respond by making a tick mark (√) against the alternative he desired. Score for each response was given as below.

The first alternative gets a score of 1, the second alternative gets a score of 2, and the third alternative gets a score of 3. This method of giving scores for the alternatives is maintained throughout the questionnaire.

Each sub-test gets a minimum score of 10 and a maximum score of 30 and the whole test gets a minimum score of 40 and a maximum score of 120. High score in a sub-test indicates high achievement motivation in that area and low score indicates a low achievement motivation in the particular area.

Questionnaire III

FLINDERS DECISION MAKING QUESTIONNAIRE-I (DMQ-I)

Based on Janis and Mann's (1977) Conflict Theory of Decision-Making, this test was designed and standardised by Mann (1982) of Flinders University, South Australia. This test was intended to measure self-esteem as a decision maker. It consists of six items. Each item is followed by three alternatives viz.

1. True for me;
2. Sometimes true for me; and
3. Not true for me.

The individual is to respond to each item by making a tick (√) against the alternative he /she desired. Each alternative of every item has its own score of 0, 1 or 2. Scoring was done according to the key prepared by the author. Thus, the test has minimum score of 0 and a maximum score of 12. High score indicates high self-esteem as a decision maker and low score indicates low self-esteem as a decision maker.

Questionnaire IV:

FLINDERS DECISION MAKING QUESTIONNAIRE – II (DMQ – II)

This test is the second part of Flinders Decision Making questionnaire. This was intended to measure the tendency to use different styles of decision making. It was validated by Burnett *et. al.*, (1989). It consists of six decision coping patterns, each measured by one sub – test namely,

1. Vigilant (V)

2. Hyper-vigilant / Panic (H)
3. Defensive avoidance (D)
4. Procrastination (P)
5. Buck passing (B)
6. Rationalisation (R)

The sub–test for vigilant decision-making style consists of six items and the other sub- tests consist of five items each. So the test consists of a total of 31 items. Items of various sub-tests are found mixed in the Questionnaire. Each item is followed by three alternatives viz.

1. True for me;
2. Sometimes true for me; and
3. Not true for me.

The subject is to respond to each item by making a tick (√) against the alternative as desired. The items are scored so as to measure strong tendencies to use the various decision coping patterns. Response to the first alternative gets a score of 0, response to the second alternative gets a score of 1 and response to the third alternative gets a score of 2.

Thus, the sub–test, vigilant decision making style, gets a minimum score of 0 and a maximum score of 12. The remaining sub-tests get a minimum score of 0 and a maximum score of 10, each. High score in one sub – test, indicates the higher tendency of the individual to follow that style. That is, the sub-scale under which an individual scores highest is the predominant decision making style of the individual.

RELIABILITY AND VALIDITY OF THE TOOLS

Even though the tools have already been validated and standardised by the respective authors, in order to test the suitability of the tools for the present sample, the tools were administered on a sample of 80 students and retest reliability was found with a time gap of 2 weeks. The following tables present the retest reliability and intrinsic validity of the tools and level of significance.

Table 4.1. Showing the Retest reliability coefficient and level of significance for DMQ-I, DMQ-II, EPQ (R) and AMS.

Sub – test	*Reliability Coefficient (N=80)*	*Test of Significance – 't' value*
DMQ – I		
Self – Esteem		
As a Decision	0.74	11.64 *
Maker		
DMQ – II		
Vigilant	0.79	11.38 *
Hypervigilant	0.47	4.70 *
Defensive		
Avoidance	0.58	6.29 *
Procrastination	0.76	10.33 *
Buck Passing	0.46	4.57 *
Rationalization	0.59	6.45 *
EPQ– R		
Extraversion	0.61	6.80 *
Neuroticism	0.81	12.20 *
Psychoticism	0.47	4.70 *
AMS		
Achievement	0.61	6.80 *
Motivation		

* $P < 0.01$

Table 4.2. Showing the Intrinsic validity coefficient and level of significance for DMQ – I, DMQ – II, EPQ(R) and AMS

Sub – test	*Validity Coefficient (N= 80)*	*Test of Significance – 't' value*
DMQ – I		
Self – Esteem		
As a Decision	0.86	14.88 *
Maker		
DMQ – II		
Vigilant	0.89	17.24 *
Hypervigilant	0.69	8.42 *
Defensive		
Avoidance	0.76	10.33 *
Procrastination	0.87	15.58 *
Buck Passing	0.68	8.19 *
Rationalization	0.77	10.66 *
EPQ (R)		
Extraversion	0.78	11.00 *
Neuroticism	0.90	18.23 *
Psychoticism	0.69	8.42 *
AMS		
Achievement	0.78	11.00 *
Motivation		

SUMMARY

The results of the validation study show that the tools are significantly reliable to the population under study. So in order to test the hypotheses the study was conducted. The data obtained have been analyzed, discussed and conclusions are drawn in the following chapter.

5

Analysis and Discussion

DESCRIPTIVE STATISTICS

The data of the study have been analysed through descriptive statistics, correlation analysis and Anova statistics. Before entering into the correlation analysis, at the outset, the general nature of the population i.e. university students with reference to the chosen variables, is analysed and discussed, through the descriptive statistics.

Table 5.1. Showing the descriptive statistics for the scores of decision making styles.

Decision making styles	*Mean*	*SD*	*Median*	*Range*	*SK*	*KU*
Vigilance	9.20	2.19	9	0-12	0.27	0.32
Hyper vigilance	5.43	2.21	5	0-10	0.59	0.26
Defensive avoidance	4.55	2.34	5	0-10	-0.57	0.28
Procrastin-ation	4.78	2.48	5	0-10	-0.25	0.26
Buck passing	4.55	2.17	5	0-10	-0.61	0.22
Rationalis-ation	5.25	2.09	5	0-10	0.36	0.24

An observation of the results of the descriptive statistics reveal that among the six decision making styles, the mean score in vigilant decision making style (9.20) is more than the mean scores in any other style,. The mean scores of the rest of the decision making styles (non-vigilant) are nearly equal. The following bar diagram represents the relative strength of six decision making styles of University students.

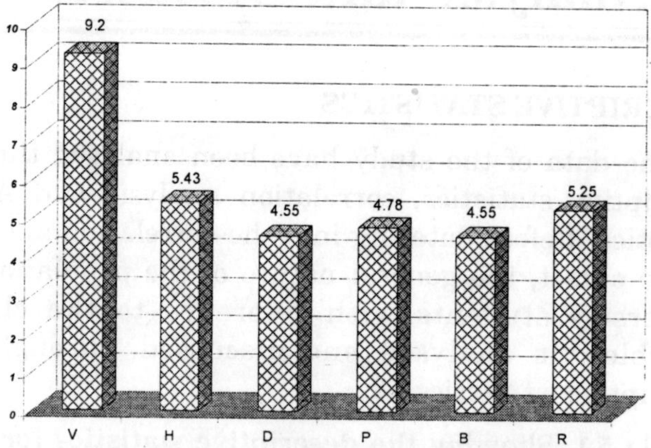

Fig. 5.1. Mean Scores in decision making styles of the sample.

The result shows that vigilant decision making styles is predominant among university students. The students are likely to be vigilant in their decisions. The mean age of the students is 21 years and they have pursued their academic studies in various educational institutions for more than 15 years. Thus, they have a good deal of experience in a wide variety of social situations. This makes the students to be vigilant in their decisions. There is a uniform deviation (SD=2) in all the decision making style scores. The skewness and kurtosis values prove that the scores in all the decision making styles are distributed normally.

Table 5.2. Showing the descriptive statistics for the scores of personality dimensions.

Personality dimension	*Mean*	*SD*	*Median*	*Range*	*SK*	*KU*
Extraversion	6.98	2.46	7	0-12	-0.04	0.36
Neuroticism	5.96	2.93	6	0-12	-0.03	0.27
Psychoticism	3.51	1.81	3	0-9	0.85	0.22

The mean scores of personality dimensions indicate that students found to have a little higher level of extraversion tendency, an average level of neuroticism tendency and very low level of psychoticism tendency.

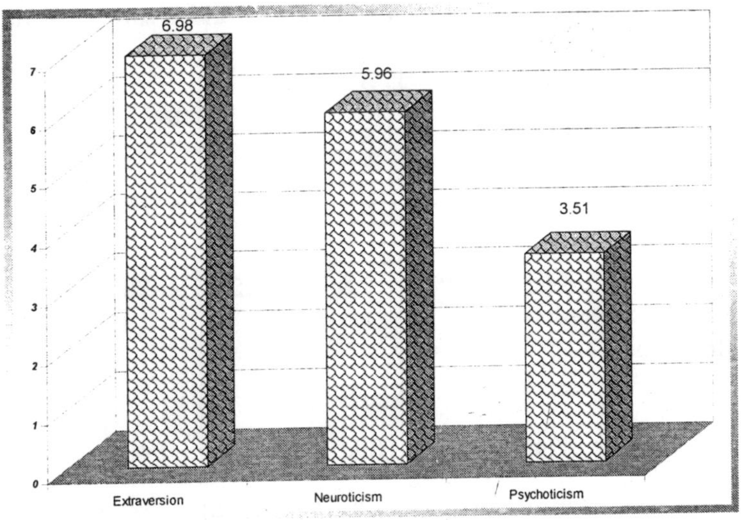

Fig. 5.2. Mean scores in personality dimensions of the sample.

The result implies that Extraversion dimension is found to be more predominant among the students than the other two dimensions. Smith Barry et.al. (1990) found that extraversion tendency increases with an increase in the age and with a wide variety of social interaction. Accordingly, the mean age of the group is 21 years and the students have all passed through various academic courses and hence have a variety of social interaction outside the family.

Individuals greatly deviate in extraversion and neuroticism dimensions when compared to psychoticism dimension. This indicates that individuals do not differ much with regard to psychoticism dimension. The result is in accordance with the result arrived at by Eysenck (1975). The skewness and kurtosis values prove that the scores in all the dimensions of personality are distributed normally.

Table 5.3. Showing the descriptive statistics of the scores of self-esteem as a decision maker and n Ach.

Variable	*Mean*	*SD*	*Median*	*Range*	*SK*	*KU*
Self-esteem as a decision maker	6.82	2.37	7.0	0-12	-0-22	0.23
n Ach	87.46	11.33	89.0	42-105	-0.40	0.25

The mean of self esteem scores is 6.82 and the skewness is –0.22. The SD (2.37) indicates that individuals differ with regard to self-esteem as decision maker. The skewness and kurtosis values indicate that scores are distributed normally.

The mean of n Ach scores is 87.46 and the skewness is –0.40. This result shows that the group as a whole has high n Ach and majority of the students in the group have scored above the group mean indicating, high n Ach. This result is in accordance with that of the result arrived at by Veroff *et. al.* (1960) wherein they found that college students have high achievement motivation.

The SD (11.33) indicates that there is wide individual differences with regard to n Ach when compared to decision self esteem. The skewness and kurtosis values indicate that the scores are distributed normally. In general, the results prove the criterion validity of the tools.

CORRELATION ANALYSIS

Through standardised tools, the levels of personality dimensions and the strength of decision making styles among the university students have been assessed and the extent of relationship between these variables were computed by Pearson Product Moment correlation statistics.

In spite of some limitations, the correlation statistics provides a coefficient to indicate the extent and the direction in which two psychological variables are related. The present study involves 11 psychological variables, viz. Extraversion, Neuroticism, Psychoticism, self-esteem as a decision maker, vigilance, hyper-vigilance, defensive avoidance, procrastination, buck passing, rationalisation, and n Ach. In order to test the major hypotheses the Pearson Product Moment correlation was computed between these psychological variables and a correlation matrix was arrived at.

Table 5.4. Showing the Correlation coefficients between Self-esteem as a decision maker and Decision making styles.

Decision making styles	*Self-esteem As a Decision maker*
Vigilance	0.2202*
Hyper vigilance	-0.5156*
Defensive avoidance	-0.4242*
Procrastination	-0.5002*
Buck passing	-0.4219*
Rationalization	-0.4363*

* P< .01

Decision making self esteem Vs vigilant decision making style:

Decision making self-esteem involves thorough understanding of the self, the values, abilities, etc. Once a person knows his/her strengths and weaknesses, he/she will make realistic decisions like considering many alternatives in light of their values. So a positive relaticnship between decision making self-esteem and vigilant style is assumed. Hence it was hypothesised that:

HY:1-1 There is a significant positive relationship between self esteem as a decision maker and vigilant decision making style.

The correlation between self-esteem as a decision maker and vigilant decision making style is 0.2202. It is significant at 0.01 level. This correlation shows that there is a significant positive relationship between self esteem as a decision maker and vigilant decision making style. Hence the stated hypothesis is accepted.

This result is in accordance with the result

obtained by Feather and Mann (1982) Govind Tiwari (1983), Distefano Pryor and Smith (1987), Mann et al (1989), Keating (1990), Burnett *et. al.* (1989) and Cheryl Ormond *et. al.* (1991). The obtained result indicates that individuals with high self esteem are vigilant in their decisions. They tend to search for more information, generate a number of alternatives and weigh them carefully considering the pros and cons, and calculating the probabilities of success before making a decision.

Decision making self esteem vs hyper vigilance decision making style:

Self esteem is the regard associated with self. Those who associate much regard to this self may not take frantic efforts to solve the problem for it would dampen the self-respect amidst others. So, a negative relationship between self-esteem as decision maker and hyper vigilance decision making style is expected. Hence it was hypothesised that :

HY:1-2 There is a signficant negative relationship between self esteem as a decision maker and hypervigilant decision making style.

The correlation between self-esteem as decision maker and hyper vigilant decision making style is –0.5156. This is significant at 0.01 level. This indicates that there is a significant negative relationship between self-esteem as decision maker and hyper vigilant decision making style. Hence the stated hypothesis is accepted. The result shows that individuals who have high self-esteem as a decision maker do not adopt hyper-vigilant style.

Self esteem as a decision maker Vs Defensive avoidance:

As self esteem is worthiness associated with the

self, individuals with high self esteem are assumed not to avoid taking a decision for want of self confidence; self reliance; self sufficiency and self dependence. So a negative relationship between self-esteem as a decision maker and defensive avoidance decision making style is assumed. Hence it was hypothesised that :

Hy:1-3 there is a significant negative relationship between self essteem as a decision maker and defensive avoidance decision making syle.

The correlation between self-esteem as decision maker and defensive avoidance is –0.4342. It is significant at 0.01 level. This result indicates that there is a significant negative relationship between self-esteem as a decision maker and defensive avoidance decision making style. Hence the stated hypothesis is accepted. The result implies that individuals with high level of self-esteem as decision maker do not adopt defensive avoidance style.

Decision making self esteem Vs procrastination

Individuals with high self esteem are confident of their own decisions. Hence they do not avoid taking a decision by procrastination. So a negative relationship between self-esteem as a decision maker and procrastination decision making style is expected. Hence it was hypothesised that :

Hy:1-4 There is a significant negative relationship between self esteem as a decision maker and procrastination decision making style.

The correlation between self-esteem as a decision maker and procrastination decision making style is –0.5002. It is significant at 0.01 level. This correlation shows that there is significant negative relationship between self-esteem as a decision maker and procrastination decision making style. Hence the stated hypothesis is accepted. The obtained result indicates that high self esteem as a decision maker inhibits procrastination decision making style. This result implies that low level of self-esteem is likely to promote procrastination style.

Decision making self esteem Vs buck passing

As self esteem implies self confidence, generally people with low self esteem may not take decisions of their own but buck pass or shift the responsibility to others. Therefore a negative relationship between self-esteem as a decision maker and buck passing is expected. So it was hypothesised that :

Hy:1-5 There is a significant negative relationship between self esteem as a decision maker and buck passing decision making style.

The correlation between self-esteem as decision maker and buck passing is –0.4219. It is significant at 0.01 level. This correlation shows that there is a significant negative relationship between self-esteem as a decision maker and buck passing. Hence the stated hypothesis is accepted. The obtained result indicates that high self esteem as decision maker inhibits buck passing decisions.

Decision making self esteem Vs rationalisation:

Individuals with high decision making self-esteem will be confident of their decision. So individuals with high self-esteem as a decision maker may not rationalize their decision. Hence it is assumed that there is a negative relationship between self-esteem as a decision maker and rationalisation decision making style. Hence it was hypothesised that :

Hy:1-6 There is a significant negative relationship between self seteem as a decision maker and rationalisation style.

The correlation between self esteem as a decision maker and rationalisation styles is –0.4363. It is significant at 0.01 level. This correlation indicates that there is significant negative relationship between self-esteem as a decision maker and rationalisation style. Hence the stated hypothesis is accepted. This result indicates that individuals having high level of self-esteem do not rationalize their decisions.

Summarising the relationship between decision self esteem and decision making styles, the results indicate that decision making self esteem is significantly positively related to vigilant style and significantly negatively related to non-vigilant styles. This result confirms the link between decision making self esteem and decision making styles proposed by Janis and Mann (1977). Other studies conducted earlier among various samples also confirms this link between decision self esteem and decision making styles (Cherryl Ormond *et. al.,* 1991 & Radford *et. al.,* 1989).

Table 5.5. Showing the Correlation coefficients between personality dimensions and Decision making styles.

Decision making styles	*Extra-version*	*Neuroticism*	*Psychoticism*
Vigilance	0.2121*	0.0011	-0.3523*
Hyper vigilance	0.0968	0.3951*	-0.0283
Defensive avoidance	-0.1269	0.3014*	0.1215
Procrastination	-0.1997*	0.2980*	0.2740*
Buck passing	-	0.1850**	0.1626
Rationalization	0.1900** -0.0428	0.2844*	0.0139

** P < .05 *P < .01

Extraversion Vs Vigilant decision making style

Out going, optimistic and sociable are some of the characteristics of extraversion. As they involve risky activities in a social setting, individuals with extraversion characteristics through higher rate of learning process (Smith Barry, 1990) in various situations may develop vigilance tendency. Hence it was hypothesised that :

Hy: 2-1-1. There is a significant positive relationship between extraversion and vigilant decision making style.

The correlation between extraversion and vigilant decision making style is 0.2121. It is significant at 0.05 level. The result shows that there is a significant positive relationship between extraversion and vigilant decision making style. Hence the stated hypothesis is accepted.

Since an extravert interacts freely with many people he/she has the advantage of acquiring information from many sources which aids in generating more alternatives and weighing those alternatives realistically. So individuals with extraversion characteristics tend to be vigilant in their decisions. The obtained result is in agreement with the findings of Richter and Tosvold (1980) and Barron and Rokeach (1983). Robinson Thomas (1990) reported that sociability and low impulsiveness is related to intrinsicness. So extraverts being characterised by sociable qualities approach a challenge not impulsively but vigilantly.

Extraversion Vs hyper vigilant decision making style

Extraverts are characterised by outgoing, optimistic, enthusiastic craving for excitement and adventurous activity. Hyper vigilant style is a decision based on contrived solution. So a negative relationship between these two variables is expected. Hence it was hypothesised that:

Hy: 2-1-2. There is a significant negative relationship between extraversion and hyper vigilant decision making style.

The correlation between extraversion and hyper vigilant decision making style is 0.0968. This is not significant. This result shows that there is no significant relationship between extraversion and hyper vigilant decision making style. Hence the stated hypothesis is rejected.

Extraversion Vs defensive avoidance decision making style

Extraverts are characterised by craving for excitement and involving in diversified activities. Defensive avoidance is the tendency of withdrawing from a decision making situation. So a negative relationship between extraversion and defensive avoidance decision making style is assumed. Hence it was hypothesised that :

Hy: 2-1-3. There is a significant negative relationship between extraversion and defensive avoidance style.

The obtained correlation between extraversion and defensive avoidance style is –0.1269. The correlation is not significant and this implies that there is no significant relationship between extraversion and defensive avoidance style. So the stated hypothesis is rejected.

Extraversion Vs Procrastination

Delaying a decision may not be a characteristic of an extravert, because an individual having extraversion tendency is active, enthusiastic and taking chance. Hence it was hypothesised that:

Hy: 2-1-4. There is a significant negative relationship between extraversion and procrastination style.

The correlation coefficient between extraversion and procrastination style is –0.1997. This is significant at 0.05 level. This shows that there is a significant negative relationship between extraversion and procrastination style. So the stated hypothesis is accepted. This result implies that individuals with extraversion characteristics do not procrastinate their decision.

Extraversion vs buck passing:

Active involvement in a variety of social situations is one of the characteristics of extraversion. So extraverts are not likely to buck pass their responsibility in making a decision. Hence a negative relationship is assumed to exist between extraversion and buck passing style. Hence it was hypothesised that:

Hy: 2-1-5. There is a significant negative relationship between extraversion and buck passing style.

The correlation between extraversion and buck passing decision making style is –0.1900. This is significant at 0.05 level. This result implies that there is a significant negative relationship between extraversion and buck passing decision making style. So the stated hypothesis is accepted. This result indicates that extraversion and buck passing are negatively related. Individuals with extraversion tendency do not buck pass their decisions.

Extraversion Vs Rationalisation style

Since an extravert is optimistic and likely to have

more sources of information, it is assumed that the extravert will not rationalize their decisions. Hence it was hypothesised that:

Hy: 2-1-6. There is a significant negative relationship between extraversion and rationalisation style

The correlation coefficient between extraversion and rationalisation style is –0.0428. This correlation is not significant. This shows that there is no significant relationship between extraversion and rationalisation style. Hence the stated hypothesis is rejected.

Neuroticism Vs Vigilant decision making style

The withdrawn nature and anxiety in neuroticism may make it difficult to decide in conflicting situation. Individuals with neuroticism tendency may not search for information and weigh the alternatives and realistically. This reasoning leads to assume that there is a significant negative relationship between neuroticism and vigilant decision making style. Hence it was hypothesised that :

Hy: 2-2-1. There is a significant negative relationship between neuroticism and vigilant decision making style

The correlation between neuroticism and vigilant decision making style is 0.0011. This is not significant indicating that there is no significant relationship between neuroticism and vigilant decision making style. Hence the stated hypothesis is rejected.

Neuroticism Vs Hyper vigilant decision making style

Some of the characteristics of neuroticism are anxiety and instability. This tendency is likely to lead to impulsive decisions. So a positive relationship between neuroticism and hyper vigilant decision styles is expected. Hence it was hypothesised that:

Hy: 2-2-2. There is a significant positive relationship between neuroticism and hyper vigilant style

The correlation coefficient between neuroticism and hyper vigilant decision making style is 0.3951. This correlation is significant at 0.01 level. This indicates that there is a significant positive relationship between neuroticism and hyper vigilant decision making style. Hence the stated hypothesis is accepted. The obtained positive correlation between neuroticism and hyper vigilant style is consistent with the result arrived at by Campbell (1981) and Radford *et. al.,* (1989). Thus there is conclusive evidence that individuals anxiety and instablity characteristics forms the basis for hypervigilant decision style.

Neuroticism Vs Defensive Avoidance Decision Making Style

The characteristic anxiety in neuroticism makes an individual to be doubtful on his / her ability to make decisions. For fear of failure, the individual may avoid making the decision itself, and defend his/her ego. Therefore possibly there can be a positive relationship between neuroticism and defensive avoidance. Hence it was hypothesised that :

Hy: 2-2-3. There is a significant positive relationship between neuroticism and defensive avoidance style

The correlation between neuroticism and defensive avoidance is 0.3014. This is significant at 0.01 level. This shows that there is a significant positive relationship between neuroticism and defensive avoidance. Hence the stated hypothesis is accepted. This result is consistent with that of the results obtained by Campbell (1981) and Radford *et.al.* (1989). This implies that individuals with high neuroticism tendency are likely to avoid making decisions and escape from decision situation.

Neuroticism Vs Procrastination

High level of anxiety dampens the performance (Yerkes Dodson, 1908). So individuals who are anxious tend to delay or put off their decisions not knowing what to do. This anxiety is likely to make his/her fearful of facing the situation. Therefore, a positive relationship between neuroticism and procrastination is expected. Hence it was hypothesised that :

Hy: 2-2-4. There is a significant positive relationship between neuroticism and procrastination style

The correlation between neuroticism and procrastination is 0.2980. It is significant at 0.01 level. This shows that there is a significant positive relationship between neuroticism and procrastination. Hence the stated hypothesis is accepted. This result is consistent with that of the result obtained by Plante Thomas *et. al.,* (1990). The result implies that individuals with neuroticism characteristics tend to procrastinate their decisions.

Neuroticism Vs Buck Passing

Neuroticism is characterised by susceptibility, or a dependence on others. So they are likely to avoid the responsibility of making decisions. So a positive relationship between neuroticism and buck passing is expected. Hence it was hypothesised that :

Hy: 2-2-5. There is a significant positive relationship between neuroticism and buck passing style

The correlation between neuroticism and buck passing is 0.1850. This is significant at 0.05 level. This result shows that there is a significant positive relationship between neuroticism and buck passing decision making style. Hence the stated hypothesis is accepted. Anxiety, the learned fear and the low level of self-esteem of neuroticism influence susceptibility which lead to buck passing. A positive correlation indicates that high level of neuroticism promotes buck passing decision making style.

Neuroticism Vs Rationalisation

Since anxiety and disowning mistakes are characteristic of neuroticism, a positive relationship is expected between neuroticism and rationalisation style. Hence it was hypothesised that :

Hy: 2-2-6. There is a significant positive relationship between neuroticism and rationalisation style

The correlation between neuroticism and rationalisation is 0.2844. This is significant at 0.01 level. This result shows that there is a significant positive relationship between neuroticism and rationalisation. Hence the stated hypothesis is accepted. The obtained result is in accordance with the findings of Olof (1990).

Psychoticism Vs Vigilant Decision

Psychoticism is characterised by not caring for people, lacking social interaction and disregard for danger and solitude. As a result individuals with psychoticism characteristics may lack information from outside. They may not generate various alternatives for a problem and weigh them realistically. That is they may not be vigilant in their decision. So, a negative relationship between psychoticism and vigilant style is expected. Hence it was hypothesised that :

Hy: 2-3-1. There is a significant negative relationship between psychoticism and vigilant style

The correlation between psychoticism and vigilant decision making style is –0.3523. This is significant at 0.01 level. This correlation shows that there is a significant negative relationship between psychoticism and vigilant decision style. Hence the stated hypothesis is accepted. This result is in accordance with that of the results obtained by Meena Sehgal (1984), wherein she found that subjects low on psychoticism were superior in vigilance, and Eysenck and Eysenck (1976) who found that high psychoticism scorers were poor in vigilance.

Psychoticism Vs Hyper Vigilant Decision

The Psychoticism tendencies as explained by Eysenck (1975) are disregard for people, insensitive etc. So, a positive relationship between Psychoticism and hyper vigilant can be expected. Hence it was hypothesised that :

Hy: 2-3-2. There is a significant positive relationship between psychoticism and hyper vigilant style

The correlation between psychoticism and hyper vigilant style is –0.083. This is not significant. This shows that there is no significant relationship between psychoticsim and hyper vigilant decision style. Hence the stated hypothesis is rejected.

Psychoticism Vs Defensive avoidance

Psychoticism is characterised by not caring for any thing, disregard for danger and solitude. A high level of these characteristics may promote defensive avoidance. So a positive relationship between these two variables is assumed. Hence it was hypothesised that :

Hy: 2-3-3. There is a significant positive relationship between psychoticism and defensive avoidance style

The correlation between psychoticism and defensive avoidance is 0.1215. This is not significant. This result shows that there is no significant relationship between psychoticism and defensive avoidance. Hence the stated hypothesis is rejected. Radford *et. al.*(1986) found that severity of psychotic disturbance (as assessed by General Psychotic disorder and Depression) was positively correlated with defensive avoidance as measured by DMQ-II. The present result does not confirm their findings.

Psychoticism vs Procrastination

People with psychoticism dimension are assumed to procrastinate due to lack of feeling disregard for danger and not caring for others. So, a positive relationship between psychoticism and procrastination is expected. Hence it was hypothesised that :

Hy: 2-3-4. There is a significant positive relationship between psychoticism and procrastination style

The correlation between psychoticism and procrastination is 0.2740. This is significant at 0.01 level. This result implies that there is a significant positive relationship between psychoticism and procrastination. So the stated hypothesis is accepted.

The result implies that students with Psychoticism

tendency more often make procrastination decision style. Probably insensitive, disregard for danger, little personal interaction (Eysenck, 1975) and suspiciousness (Sing 1978) nature of psychoticism dimension of personality would make them to adopt procrastination decision making style.

Psychoticism Vs Buck Passing

Hostility and not caring for others (even to his own kith and kin) are some of the characteristics of psychoticism. So at the time of crisis or conflicting situations they may shift the responsibility of making decisions to others. Hence a positive relationship between psychoticism and buck passing is expected. Hence it was hypothesised that :

Hy: 2-3-5. There is a significant positive relationship between psychoticism and buck passing style

The correlation between psychoticism and buck passing is 0.1626. This is not a significant correlation. This result shows that there is no significant relationship between psychoticism and buck passing. Therefore the stated hypothesis is rejected.

Psychoticism Vs Rationalisation

As psychoticism dimension of personality is characterised by aggressive, hostility and disregard for danger individuals with psychoticism tendency may rationalize the decisions. Hence a positive relationship between psychoticism and rationalisation decision style is expected. Hence it was hypothesised that :

Hy: 2-3-6 There is a significant positive relationship between psychoticism and rationalisation style

The correlation between psychoticism and rationalisation is 0.0139. This is not significant. This result indicates that the relationship between psychoticsim and rationalisation decision style is not significant. Hence the stated hypothesis is accepted.

Table 5-6. Showing the correlation coefficients between achievement motivation and decision making styles

Decision making style	*n Ach*
Vigilance	0.2333*
Hyper Vigilance	-0.0433
Defensive avoidance	-0.0780
Procrastination	-0.0114
Buck passing	-0.0654
Rationalization	-0.1096

Achievement motivation Vs Vigilant decision making style:

High Achievers, according to Atkinson (1978), consider various aspects towards their success like probability of success and pros and cons and carefully decide to take a middling choice. According to the author of DMQ, this forms the basis for a vigilant decision making. So a positive relationship between n Ach and vigilant decision style is expected. Hence it was hypothesised that :

Hy: 3.1. There is a significant positive relationship between n ach and vigilant style

The correlation between n Ach and vigilant decision making style is 0.2333. It is significant at 0.01 level. The result indicates that there is a significant positive relationship between n Ach and vigilant decision making style. Hence the stated hypothesis is accepted. The result is consistent with that of the results arrived at by Rim (1963), Zamft Hyman (1975) and Slade *et. al.* (1991).

Achievement motivation vs hyper-vigilant decision making style:

As high achievers are conscious about the choice they select, they may not be hyper vigilant in their decisions. Hence a negative relationship is expected between n Ach and hyper vigilant decision making style. So, it was hypothesised that:

Hy: 3-2 There is a significant negative relationship between n ach and hyper-vigilant style.

The correlation between n Ach and hyper-vigilant style is -0.0433. This correlation is not significant. This result shows that n Ach is not significantly related to hyper vigilant style. Hence the stated hypothesis is rejected.

Achievement Motivation vs Defensive Avoidance

During confilicting situations, high achievers approach the problem by taking a middling choice. They may not avoid taking a decision. Therefore a negative relationship between n Ach and defensive avoidance is assumed. Hence it was hypothesised that:

Hy:3-3 There is a significant negative relationship between n ach and defensive avoidance.

The correlation between n Ach and defensive avoidance is –0.0786. This is not significant. This shows that there is no significant relationship between n Ach and defensive avoidance. Hence the stated hypothesis is rejected.

Achievement Motivation vs Procrastination

Achievement behaviours are ongoing process. So, a negative relationship is assumed between achievement motivation and procrastination. Hence it was hypothesised that:

Hy:3-4 There is a significant negative relationship between n ach and procrastination.

The correlation between Ach and procrastination style is –0.0114. This is not a significant correlation. This result shows that there is no significant relationship between n Ach and procrastination decision style. Hence the stated hypothesis is rejected.

Achievement motivation vs Buck Passing

High Achievers have a tendency to set an optimum goal and wish to attain that level by their own efforts. So, a negative relationship is expected between n Ach and buck passing decision style. Hence it was hypothesised that

Hy:3-5 There is a Significant Negative Relationship between n Ach and Buck Passing

The correlation between n Ach and buck passing is 0.0654. This is not significant. This shows that there is no significant relationship between n Ach and buck passing decision style. Hence the stated hypothesis is rejected.

Achievement Motivation Vs Rationalisation

As high achievers are characterised by goal oriented and not giving reasons for their failure thereof, a negative relationship between n Ach and rationalisation is expected. Hence it was hypothesised that:

Hy:3-6 There is a significant negative relationship between n ach and rationalisation.

The correlation between n Ach and rationalisation is –0.1096. This is not a significant correlation, which shows that there is no significant relationship between n Ach and rationalisation. Hence the stated hypothesis is rejected.

To sum our discussion with regard to the relationship between achievement motivation and decision making styles, the results in Table 5.6 confirms the relationship between decision making styles and achievement motivation. There is a significant positive relationship between vigilant decision making and achievement motivation. The result indicates that vigilant decision making skills are associated with their level of achievement motivation. Individuals with relatively high level of achievement motivation are more often found to make vigilant decision making style. These individuals may be careful enough to collect relevant information pertaining to the problem and generate many alternatives and weigh those alternatives (the pros and cons of each alternative) to take a quality decision. The study revealed that there is no significant relationship between non-vigilant decision making styles and achievement motivation.

Table 5.7. Showing the Correlation coefficients between personality dimensions and self-esteem as a decision maker.

Personality Dimensions	*Self – esteem as a decision maker*
Extraversion	0.0292
Neuroticism	-0.3598*
Psychoticism	-0.0834

*p<.01

Extraversion Vs Self–esteem as a Decision Maker

Since an extravert is an outgoing and optimistic person, he is likely to have exposure to a variety of social situations in life. This experience should lead to higher probability of success and consequently to a high level of self–esteem. Hence it was hypothesised that

Hy: 4-1 There is a significant positive relaitonship between extraversion and self - esteem as a decision maker

The correlation between Extraversion and Self-esteem as a decision maker is 0.0292. This is not a significant correlation. This shows that there is no significant relationship between extraversion and self-esteem as a decision maker. Hence the stated hypothesis is rejected.

Neuroticism Vs Self–esteem as a Decision Maker

Neuroticism is characterised by withdrawn, narrow range of involvement, cautious, and instability caused by anxiety. These characteristics are generally believed to demote self-esteem. So, a negative relationship between neuroticism and self – esteem as a decision maker is expected. Hence it was hypothesised that:

Hy: 4-2 There is a significant negative relationship between neuroticism and self-esteem as a decision maker.

The correlation between Neuroticism and self–esteem as a decision maker is – 0.3598. This is significant at 0.01 level. This indicates that there is a significant negative relationship between Neuroticism and self – esteem as a decision maker. Hence the stated hypothesis is accepted.

The result indicates that there is a significant negative correlation between Neuroticism and decision making self-esteem. This is in accordance with the findings of Brown (1990), Wolfe Raymond *et. al.* (1990) and Nichols Hoppe *et. al.* (1990). The result implies that individuals with neuroticism tendency have low level of self esteem as a decision maker.

Psychoticism Vs Self–esteem as a decision maker:

The characteristic of psychoticism dimension is being solitary. But self-esteem is the learned sense of personal worth received from others. So a negative relationship between psychoticim and Self–esteem as a decision maker is assumed. Hence it was hypothesized that :

Hy: 4-3 There is a significant negative relationship between psychoticism and self-esteem as a decision maker

The correlation between psychoticism and self – esteem as a decision maker is –0.0834. This is not significant. This shows that there is no significant relationship between psychoticism and self–esteem as a decision maker. Hence the stated hypothesis is rejected.

Table 5-8. Showing the Correlation coefficient between Achievement Motivation and self- esteem as a decision maker.

	n Ach	*Level of Significance*
Self–esteem as a Decision maker	0.0990	NS

Achievement Motivation vs Self–esteem as a decision maker

Achievement motivation is characterised by the selection of an optimum task difficulty which is possible only by a realistic appraisal of one's previous accomplishments. So a positive relationship between n

Ach and Self–esteem as a decision maker is expected. Hence it was hypothesised that:

Hy: 5 There is a significant positive relationship between n Ach and self-esteem as a decision maker.

The correlation between n Ach and self–esteem as a decision maker is 0.0990. This is not a significant correlation. This implies that there is no significant relationship between n Ach and Self–esteem as a decision maker. Hence the stated hypothesis is rejected.

Table 5-9. Showing the Correlation coefficients between personality dimension and Achievement motivation.

Personality Dimensions	*n Ach*
Extraversion	0.0539
Neuroticism	-0.0235
Psychoticism	-0.2044*

*p<.05

Extraversion Vs n Ach

As Extraversion is associated with low level of arousal (Eysenck, 1967), they seek strange, novel and exciting situation and n Ach is also characterised by achieving newer things. So a positive correlation is expected between extraversion and n Ach. Hence it was hypothesised that :

Hy: 6-1 There is a significant positive relationship between extraversion and n Ach

The correlation between Extraversion and n Ach is 0.0539. It is not significant. This shows that there is no significant relationship between Extraversion and n Ach. Hence the stated hypothesis is rejected.

Neuroticism Vs n Ach

Susceptibility, impulsivity and instability are the predominant characteristics of Neuroticism. These characteristics imply that persons with neuroticism tendency may not bother about quality of performance while quality is the main characteristic of n Ach. Moreover, anxiety a characteristic of Neuroticism (Eysenck, 1967), is a motive to avoid failure (Atkinson, et. al.1960). So a negative relationship between Neuroticism and n Ach is expected. Hence it was hypothesised that:

Hy: 6-2 There is a significant negative relationship between neuroticism and n Ach

The correlation between Neuroticism and n Ach is –0.0235. This is not a significant correlation. This result indicates that there is no significant relationship between Neuroticism and achievement motivation. Hence the stated hypothesis is rejected. This result indicates that Neuroticism is not related to n Ach. This is consistent with that of the result arrived at by Ray (1990).

Psychoticism vs n Ach

Solitary, not caring for people, hostile and aggressiveness are characteristics of psychoticism. As these characteristics are not helpful for achievement, a negative relationship between psychoticism and n Ach is expected. Hence it was hypothesised that:

Hy: 6-3 There is a significant negative relationship between psychoticism and n Ach

The correlation between psychoticism and n Ach is –0.2044. This negative correlation is significant at 0.05 level. This indicates that there is a significant negative relationship between psychoticism and n Ach. Hence the stated hypothesis is accepted. The result confirms the result already arrived at by Pearson Paul *et. al.* (1989) wherein they found that psychoticism is associated with little purpose in life. So the result makes it clear that individuals with high level of psychoticism tendency do not achieve great things.

3. t-TESTS COMPARING MALES AND FEMALES

In order to test the sub-hypotheses with regard to gender differences two randomised group design was used. The results are tabulated and discussed hereunder.

HO: 1 There is no significant difference between males and females with regard to self-esteem as a decision maker.

Table 5.10 shows the Mean, SD, SED, CR and the level of significance for scores of males and females in DMQ-I. The obtained CR for self-esteem as a decision maker scores of males and females is significant at .05 level. Hence the stated null hypothesis is rejected.

This result indicates that males have a higher self – esteem as a decision maker than females. This is probably because males are given more freedom and opportunities to make decisions in our society. The wide range of involvement in the society and the experience in a variety of situations of males when compared to females cause males to attach more regard with their selves. This result is consistent with the previous findings (e.g. Mann *et. al.* 1989, and Cheryl Ormond *et. al.* 1991). These authors found that males have higher level of decision self-esteem than females.

HO: 2 There is no significant diference between males and females with regard to decision making styles.

Table 5.10. Showing the Means, SDs, SED, CR and the level of significance for scores of Males and Females in Self–esteem as a decision maker (DMQ-I)

Mean		*Standard Deviation*		*Standard Error*	*Cr*	*Level of Significance*
Males (n=63)	*Females (n=51)*	*Males*	*Females*			
7.127	6.451	2.282	2.460	0.449	1.5066	0.05

Table. 5.11 Showing the Means, SDs, SEDs, CRS and the level of significance for scores of males and females in decision making styles (DMQ-II)

Decision making styles	*Mean* *Males*	*Female*	*Standard Deviation*		*Standard Error*	*Cr*	*Level of Signi-ficance*
	(n=63)	*(n=51)*	*Males*	*Females*			
Vigilant	9.63	9.27	2.32	2.04	0.27	0.75	Ns
Hyper vigilant	5.20	5.25	2.20	2.21	0.41	1.24	Ns
Defensive Avoidance	4.50	4.60	0.50	2.14	0.42	0.29	Ns
Procrastination	4.69	4.90	2.31	2.68	0.47	0.42	Ns
Buck passing	4.44	4.68	1.99	2.38	0.41	0.57	Ns
Rationalisation	5.39	5.07	2.09	2.10	0.39	0.80	Ns

Table. 5.12. Showing the Mean, SDs, SEDs, CR and the level of significance for scores of Males and females in personality dimensions.

Personality Dimensions	*Mean*		*Standard Deviation*		*Standard Error*	*Cr*	*Level of Signi-Ficance*
	Males (n=63)	*Female (n=51)*	*Males*	*Females*			
Extraversion	6.92	7.02	2.35	2.61	0.47	0.21	Ns
Neuroticism	5.95	5.98	2.88	3.03	0.55	0.05	Ns
Psychoticism	3.63	3.37	1.74	1.90	0.34	0.75	Ns

Table. 5-13. Showing the Means, SDs, SED, CR and the level of significance for n Ach Scores of Males and females.

Mean		*Standard Deviation*		*Standard Error*	*Cr*	*Level of Significance*
Males (n=63)	*Ffemale (n=51)*	*Males*	*Females*			
87.00	88.02	13.49	7.96	2.03	0.05	Ns

Table 5.11 shows the Means, SDs, SEDs, CRs and the level of significance for scores of male and females in decision making styles (DMQ-II). The obtained CRs are not significant. Hence the stated null hypothesis is accepted. The result indicates that males and females do not differ with regard to decision making styles. This result confirms the result arrived at by Cherry1 Ormond *et. al.* (1991) wherein they found no difference between males and females in Decision metacognitive knowledge or in their performance on the scenario.

HO: 3 There is no significant difference between males and females with regard to personality dimensions.

The Table 5.12 shows the Mean, SDs, SEDs, CRs and the level of significance for scores of males and females in personality dimensions. The obtained CRs for the three personality dimensions are not significant. Hence the stated null hypothesis is accepted. This result indicates that there is no sex difference with regard to personality dimensions, viz. Extraversion, Neuroticism and psychoticism.

HO: 4 There is no significant difference between males and females with regard to n ach.

Table 5.13 shows the Means, SDs, SED, CR and the level of significance of n Ach scores of males and females. The obtained CR is not significant. Hence the stated null hypothesis is accepted. This result indicates that there is no sex difference with regard to n Ach. This result is in agreement with the findings of Maccoby and Jacklin, et.al. (1974), who found that most consistent finding on sex difference is that there are really very few sex differences.

To sum the results with regard to sex difference on the psychological variables, it is found that males and females do not differ in personality dimensions, decision making styles and achievement motivation. Only in decision self-esteem the sex difference is found. It was found that males are superior in decision self-esteem than females.

As earlier studies established the link between decision self-esteem and vigilant decision making style, the result that males are superior on decision self-esteem than females but not in vigilant decision making style is a discrepancy. Similar discrepancy had already arrived at by Cherryl Ormond *et. al.*(1991). They found that there was a curious (and unwarranted) discrepancy between female's knowledge and performance on decision tasks and self – concept as a decision maker. Crandall (1969) found that males tend to overestimate their future success relative to their ability level and Gurman Ernest *et. al.* (1990) found that over estimators had significantly higher Self–esteem. These results provide an alternative interpretation to the sex difference that males have higher level of decision self-esteem than females. In fact, women have a realistic awareness of their limitations whereas men tend to overestimate their capabilities and have an inaccurate self perception. This would have led to a condition that males to have a high level of self – esteem as a decision maker when compared to females. However, future studies have to be conducted to ponder over this discrepancy further.

4. t-Tests comparing professional course students and non-professional course students

Through two randomised group design the differences between professional course students and Non-professional course students with respect to the chosen variables have been analysed. The results are as follow.

Table 5.14. Showing the Means, SDs, SED, CR and the level of significance for scores of Professional and non-professional course students in self – esteem as a decision Maker (DMQ-I).

Mean *Prof.*	*Non-prof.*	*Standard Deviation*		*Standard Error*	*Cr*	*Level of Significance*
(n=67)	*(n=47)*	*Prof.*	*Non-prof.*			
6.79	6.87	2.44	2.30	0.45	0.18	Ns

Note: - Prof. - Professional course students

Non-pro. - Non-professional course students.

Table 5.15. Showing the Means, SDs, SEDs, CRs and the level of significance for scores of professional and non-professional course students in Decision making styles (DMQ – II)

Decision making styles	*Mean* *Prof.*	*Non-prof.*	*Standard Deviation*		*Standard Error*	*Cr*	*Level of Signi-ficance*
	(n=57)	*(n=47)*	*Prof*	*Non-prof.*			
Vigilant	9.37	8.95	2.31	2.02	0.40	1.02	Ns
Hyper vigilant	5.39	5.51	2.46	1.85	0.40	0.30	Ns
Defensive Avoidance	4.21	5.04	2.35	2.27	0.44	1.90	Ns
Procrastination	4.52	5.17	2.55	2.29	0.46	1.41	Ns
Buck passing	4.55	4.55	0.26	2.06	0.40	0.01	Ns
Rationalisation	5.62	4.72	2.03	2.10	0.39	2.29.	0.05

HO: 5 There is no significant difference between professional course students and non-professional course students with regard to self–esteem as a decision maker.

From the Table 5.14 the difference in means is not significant. Hence the stated null hypothesis is accepted. This result indicates that professional course students and Non-professional course students do not differ with regard to decision making self-esteem.

HO: 6 There is no significant difference between professional course students and non-professional course students with regard to decision making styles.

From the Table 5.15 the differences in means are not significant except in Rationalisation. So, the stated null hypothesis is accepted except for Rationalisation. The results indicate that professional course students and non-professional course students do not differ in their decision making styles except in rationalisation. Professional course students have more rationalising tendency than Non-professional course students.

HO: 7 There is no significant difference between professional course students and non-professional course students with regard to personality dimensions.

Table 5.16 shows the scores of professional course students and Non-Professional course students in the three personality dimensions. The difference in means is not significant with regard to Extraversion. But the difference in means is significant with regard to Neuroticism ($P<0.05$) and psychoticism ($P<0.05$). The result indicates that professional course students, and Non-Professional course students do not differ in Extraversion dimension. But, they differ in neuroticism

Table 5.16. showing the Means, SDs, SEDs, CRs and the level of significance for scores of professional and non-professional course students in personality dimensions

Personality Dimensions	*Mean*		*Standard Deviation*		*Standard Error*	*Cr*	*Level of Significance*
	Prof.	*Non-pro.*					
	(n=67)	*(n=47)*	*Prof*	*Non-prof*			
Extraversion	6.97	6.95	2.60	2.27	0.46	0.02	Ns
Neuroticism	6.43	5.29	2.75	3.07	0.56	0.02	0 .05
Psychoticism	3.23	3.91	1.78	1.80	1.80	0.34	0.05

Table 5.17. Showing the Means, SDs. SED, CRs and the level of significance for n Ach scores of professional and non-professional course students.

Mean		*Standard Deviation*		*Standard Error*	*Cr*	*Level of Significance*
Prof.	*Non-pro.*					
(n=67)	*(n=47)*	*Prof.*	*Non-pro.*			
85.60	90.11	12.8	8.03	1.96	2.29	.05

and psychoticism. Professional course students have significantly higher level of Neuroticism whereas Non-professional course students have significantly higher level of psychoticism.

HO: 8 There is no significant difference between professional course students and non-professional course students with regard to n ach

Table 5.17 shows the scores of professional course students and Non-professional course students in n Ach. The difference in mean is significant at .05 level. Hence the stated null hypothesis is rejected. This result indicates that Non- professional course students have higher achievement motivation when compared to professional course students.

The reasons probably are: (1) Non-professional course students have to compete with a large number of people to achieve their goal especially in job opportunity, (2) The professional course students have chosen a specific field within which the competition is less compared to Non- professional course students.

Summarising the results with regard to the difference between professional course students and non-professional course students, in the present study, it was found that professional course students have more Neuroticism tendency when compared to Non-professional course students. Professional course students have chosen a specific field for their study. Hence, they are likely to have a narrow range of involvement. So, they avoid taking decision, not by procrastination or buck passing, instead they rationalize their decisions. This assumption was confirmed by a significant positive correlation (0.2844) between Neuroticism and Rationalisation. It was also found that, professional course students are low

Table 5.18. Showing the Means, SDs, SEMs for the three levels of Birth order groups on Decision making self-esteem scores.

S.No	*Birth order Groups*	*N*	*Mean*	*Sd*	*Sem*
1.	1st Borns	51	6.333	2.511	0.3516
2.	2nd Borns	30	7.433	2.388	0.4360
3.	Later Borns	33	6.939	2.014	0.3506

Table 5.19. Showing the summary of analysis of Variance for the three levels of Birth Order groups on Decision Making Self-esteem scores.

Source Variation	*Sum of Square*	*Df*	*Mean Square*	*F-Ratio*	*Level of Significance*
BSS	23.7809	2	11.8904		
WSS	610.5788	111	5.5008	2.1617	NS
TSS	634.3597	113			

achievers. As they are less likely to be motivated they may rationalize their decisions.

5. F TESTS COMPARING FIRST BORNS, SECOND BORNS AND LATER BORNS

The differences among different ordinal position with respect to the psychological variables chosen have been tested using more than two randomised group design. The results are tabulated and discussed.

HO: 9 There is no significant difference among the students of different orders of birth with regard to self-esteem as a decision maker.

Table 5.18 shows the Means, SDs, SEMs, for three levels of birth order groups on decisions making self-esteem scores. Table 5.19 shows the summary of analysis of variance for the three levels of birth order groups viz. 1st borns, 2nd borns and later borns, on decision making self-esteem scores. The obtained F value is 2.1617. It is not significant. Hence the stated null hypothesis is accepted. This result indicates that ordinal positions have no effect on decision making self-esteem of individuals.

HO: 10 There is no significant difference between students of different orders of birth with regard to decision making styles.

The results of ANOVA in Table 5.31 reveal that there is significant difference among the three levels of birth order groups with regard to nationalisation decision styles. In order to find out the two levels, which significantly differ, a pair-wise comparison was made and the results are as follows.

Table 5.32 ahead shows the level of significance of the difference in the mean scores of first borns and second borns in Rationalisation. The difference is

Table 5.20. Showing the Means, SDs, SEMs, for the three levels of Birth order groups on Vigilant Scores.

S. No	*Birth order Groups*	*N*	*Mean*	*Sd*	*Sem*
1.	1st Borns	51	9.196	2.417	0.3384
2.	2nd Borns	30	9.333	1.988	0.3630
3.	Later Borns	33	9.090	2.082	0.3624

Table 5.21. Showing the summary of analysis of Variance for the three levels of Birth order groups on Vigilant Scores.

Source Variation	*Sum of Square*	*Df*	*Mean Square*	*F-Ratio*	*Level of Significance*
BSS	0.926439	2	0.4632		
WSS	545.433156	111	4.9139	0.0942	NS
TSS	546.359649	113			

Table 5.22. Showing the Means, SDs, SEMs, for the three levels of Birth order groups on Hyper Vigilant Scores.

S. No	*Birth order Groups*	*N*	*Mean*	*Sd*	*Sem*
1.	1st Borns	51	5.706	2.184	0.3058
2.	2nd Borns	30	5.000	2.477	0.4522
3.	Later Borns	33	5.424	2.016	0.3509

Table 5.23. Showing the summary of analysis of Variance for the three levels of Birth order groups on Hyper Vigilant Scores.

Source Variation	*Sum of Square*	*Df*	*Mean Square*	*F-Ratio*	*Level of Significance*
BSS	9.4213	2	4.7107	0.9565	NS
WSS	546.6488	111	4.9248		
TSS	556.0701	113			

Table 5.24. Showing the Mean, SDs, SEMs, for the three levels of Birth order groups on Defensive Avoidance Scores

S. No	*Birth order Groups*	*N*	*Mean*	*Sd*	*Sem*
1.	1st Borns	51	4.608	2.530	0.3543
2.	2nd Borns	30	4.233	2.515	0.4592
3.	Later Borns	33	5.121	1.883	0.3278

able 5.25. Showing the summary of analysis of Variance for three levels or Birth order groups on Defensive Avoidance Scores

Source Variation	*Sum of Square*	*Df*	*Mean Square*	*F-ratio*	*Level of Significance*
BSS	12.6191	2	6.3097		
WSS	617.0388	111	5.5590	1.1350	NS
TSS	629.6579	113			

Table 5.26. Showing the Means. SDs, SEMs, for the three levels of Birth order groups on Procrastination Scores

S. No	*Birth Order Groups*	*N*	*Mean*	*SD*	*SEM*
1.	1st Borns	51	4.608	2.616	0.3666
2.	2nd Borns	30	4.900	2.523	0.4606
3.	Later Borns	33	4.970	2.271	0.3953

Table 5.27. Showing the summary of analysis of Variance for the three levels of Birth order groups on Procrastination Scores

Source Variation	*Sum of Square*	*Df*	*Mean Square*	*F-Ratio*	*Level of Significance*
BSS	3.1208	2	1.5604		
WSS	691.8266	111	6.2327	0.2503	NS
TSS	694.9474	113			

Table 5.28. Showing the Means, SDs, SEMs, for the three levels of Birth order groups on Buck Passing Scores

S. No	*Birth Order Groups*	*N*	*Mean*	*SD*	*SEM*
1.	1st Borns	51	4.647	2.207	0.30903
2.	2nd Borns	30	4.367	2.580	0.4710
3.	Later Borns	33	4.576	1.714	0.2984

Table 5.29. Showing the summary of analysis of Variance for the three levels of Birth order group on Buck Passing Scores

Source Variation	*Sum of Square*	*Df*	*Mean Square*	*F-Ratio*	*Level of Significance*
BSS	1.5098	2	0.7550		
WSS	530.6744	111	4.7809	0.1580	NS
TSS	532.1842	113			

Table 5.30. Showing the Means, SDs, SEMs, for the three levels of Birth order groups on Rationalisation Scores

S.No	*Birth Order Groups*	*N*	*Mean*	*SD*	*SEM*
1.	1st Borns	51	5.824	2.076	0.2907
2.	2nd Borns	30	4.633	2.498	0.4561
3.	Later Borns	33	4.939	1.478	0.2573

Table 5.31. Showing the summary of analysis of Variance for the three levels of Birth order on Rationalisation Scores

Source Variation	*Sum of Square*	*Df*	*Mean Square*	*F-Ratio*	*Level of Significance*
BSS	31.3656	2	15.6828		
WSS	466.2573	111	4.2005	3.7335	.05
TSS	497.6229	113			

Table 5.32. Showing the Means, SDs, SED, CR and the level of significance for Rationalisation scores of first borns and second borns

Mean		*Standard Deviation*		*Standard Error*	*CR*	*Level of Significance*
First Borns (n=51)	*Second Borns (n=30)*	*First Borns*	*Second Borns*			
5.824	4.633	2.076	2.498	0.5408	2.2023	0.05

Table 5.33. Showing the Means, SDs, SED, CR and the level of significance for Rationalisation scores of first borns and later borns

Mean		*Standard Deviation*		*Standard Error*	*CR*	*Level of Significance*
First Borns (n=51)	*Later Borns (n=33)*	*First Borns*	*Later Borns*			
5.824	4.939	2.076	1.478	0.3882	2.2798	0.05

Table 5.34.. Showing the Mean, SD, SED, CR and the level of significance for Rationalisation scores of second borns and later borns.

Mean		*Standard Deviation*		*Standard Error*	*CR*	*Level of Significance*
Second Borns (n=30)	*Later Borns (n=33)*	*Second Borns*	*Later Borns*			
4.633	4.939	2.498	1.478	0.5236	0.5844	NS

significant at 0.05 level, indicating that first borns have more rationalizsng tendency than second borns.

Table 5.33 shows the level of significance of the difference in the mean scores of first borns and later borns in Rationalisation style. The difference is significant at 0.05 level, indicating that first borns have more rationalising tendency than later borns.

Table 5.34 shows the level of significance of the difference in the mean scores of second borns and late borns in Rationalisation. The difference is not significant. The result indicates that there is no significant difference between second borns and later borns in rationalising tendency.

The following bar diagram represents the relative strength of rationalising tendency of the three birth order groups.

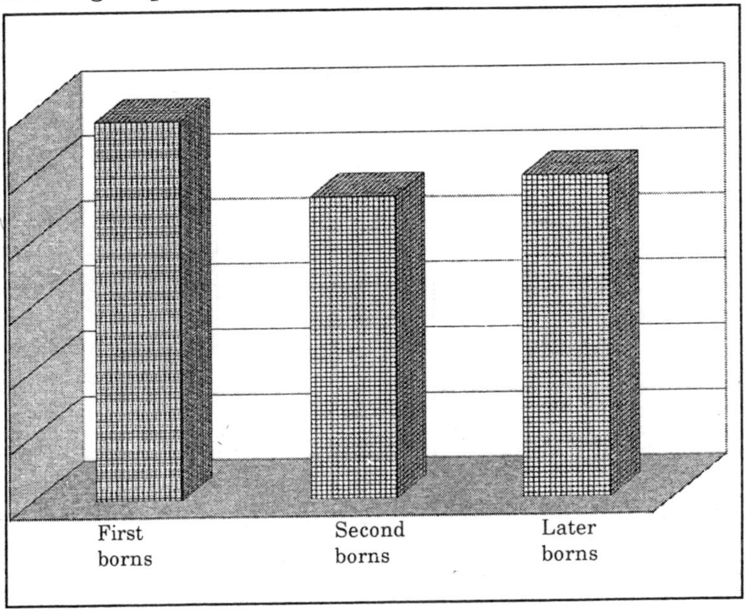

Fig 5.3. Mean scores of Rationalisation decision among birth order groups.

Table 5.35. Showing the Means, SDs, SEMs, for the three levels of birth order Groups on Extraversion scores.

S. No	*Birth Order Groups*	*N*	*Mean*	*SD*	*SEM*
1.	1st Borns	51	7.392	2.228	0.3119
2.	2nd Borns	30	6.533	2.258	0.4615
3.	Later Borns	33	6.697	2.710	0.4717

Table 5.36. Showing the summary of analysis of Variance for the three levels of birth order groups on Extraversion Scores.

Source Variation	*Sum of Square*	*Df*	*Mean Square*	*F-Ratio*	*Level of Significance*
BSS	14.8979	2	7.4490		
WSS	629.0933	111	5.6675	1.3143	NS
TSS	643.9912	113			

Table 5.37. Showing the Means, SDs, SEMs, for the three levels of birth order groups on Neuroticism Scores.

S. No	*Birth Order Groups*	*N*	*Mean*	*SD*	*SEM*
1.	1st Borns	51	5.960	2.856	0.3999
2.	2nd Borns	30	5.733	2.863	0.5227
3.	Later Borns	33	6.182	3.186	0.5546

Table. 5.38. Showing the summary of analysis of Variance for the three levels of birth order groups on Neuroticism Scores.

Source Variation	*Sum of Square*	*Df*	*Mean Square*	*F-Ratio*	*Level of Significance*
BSS	3.1622	2	1.5811	0.1808	NS
WSS	970.6974	111	8.7450		
TSS	973.8596	113			

Table 5.39. **Showing the Mean, SDs, SEMs, for the three levels of birth order groups on Psychoticism Scores.**

S. No.	*Birth Order Groups*	*N*	*Mean*	*SD*	*SEM*
1.	1st Borns	51	3.471	1.671	0.2339
2.	2nd Borns	30	3.030	1.771	0.3233
3.	Later Borns	33	4.030	2.023	0.3521

Table 5.40. **Showing the summary of analysis of Variance for the three levels of birth order groups on Psychoticism Scores.**

Source Variation	*Sum of Square*	*Df*	*Mean Square*	*F-Ratio*	*Level of Significance*
BSS	15.8226	2	7.9114	2.4623	Ns
WSS	356.6423	111	3.2130		
TSS	372.4649	113			

From the above three results, it is concluded that first borns have significantly more rationalising tendency than second borns and later borns. Studies reveal that first borns tend to conform to adult standards (Hilton, 1967) and to the social pressures (Sampson, 1967) than later borns. In order to cope with the conformity, first borns may rationalize their decisions.

HO: 11 There is no significant difference between students of different orders of birth with regard to personality dimensions.

Tables 5.35 to 5.40 show the ANOVA for the three levels of birth order groups on Personality dimensions. None of the differences in means is significant. Hence the stated null hypothesis is accepted. This result indicates that students of different ordinal positions do not differ in any of the personality dimensions.

Studies conducted earlier on personality dimensions reveal an inconsistent result with regard to birth order. George et.al. (1975) reported the influence of birth order on Extraversion but not on Neuroticism. Vithal Rao Yadav (1988) reported that birth order influences on Neuroticism but not on Extraversion. The present study reveals that none of these two personality dimensions is influenced by birth order.

HO: 12 There is no significant difference between students of different orders of birth with regard to n ach.

Table 5.41 shows the Means, SDs, SEDs, for the three levels of Birth order groups on Achievement motivation scores. Table 5.42 shows the summary of analysis of Variance for the three levels of Birth order groups viz. 1st borns, 2nd borns and later borns. The F

Table 5.41. Showing the Means, SDs, SEMs, for the three levels of birth order Groups on n Ach Scores.

S. No.	*Birth Order Groups*	*N*	*Mean*	*SD*	*SEM*
1.	1st Borns	51	88.00	10.210	1.4297
2.	2nd Borns	30	87.10	7.862	1.4354
3.	Later Borns	33	86.242	16.386	2.8524

Table 5.42. Showing the summary of analysis of Variance for the three levels of birth order groups on n Ach Scores.

Source Variation	*Sum of Square*	*Df*	*Mean Square*	*F-Ratio*	*Level of Significance*
BSS	62.8622	2	31.4311	0.2237	Ns
WSS	15,596.7606	111	140.5113		
TSS	15,659.6228	113			

value obtained (0.2237) is not significant. Hence the stated null hypothesis is accepted. This result indicates that Birth order does not have an influence on n Ach.

SUMMARY

The present study reveals that there is a positive relationship between extraversion and vigilant decision making style. Students with extraversion dimension of personality are more often found to adopt vigilant decision making style. Extraverts are characterised by outgoing and sociable tendencies (Esenck and Eysenck, 1963). They may interact with many people freely and acquire more information and practice (Crowmwell, 1963; Rotter 1966 and Seeman, *et. al.,* 1963) from many sources. They habituate those information (Smith Barry, 1990) generate more alternatives, interpret (evaluating) the alternatives and make judgments based on the world outside themselves (realistically). Finally they may make commitments with confidence (Thibaut and Kelly, 1959).

Thus, the students with extraversion tendency must perceive the situation in a wider perspective and with sufficient consideration into future consequences involve in vigilant decision making style – a decision of high quality of information processing.

The result that vigilant decision making style significantly correlates with extraversion (outgoing and sociable) tendencies and psychoticism (solitary and little personal interaction) tendencies (Table 5.5) may be interpreted as acquiring more information in the social context is the necessary condition for vigilant decision making style.

The extraversion characteristics are also found to inhibit non-vigilant decision making styles like procrastination and buck passing decision making styles. That is students with extraversion characteristics do not make procrastination and buck passing decision styles.

The present study reveals that there is no significant relationship between extraversion and decision self esteem. When extraversion significantly correlates with vigilance decision making style, it does not correlate with decision self esteem. So evidence is not found in the present study that extraversion tendency promotes vigilant decision making style via decision making self esteem.

Similarly evidence is not found in the present study to claim that extraversion promotes vigilant decision style via achievement motivation. Thus there is no evidence that in the case of extraversion dimension of personality, neither decision self esteem nor achievement motivation function as mediating variable to promote vigilance.

Consistent with earlier studies (Campbell, 1981) the present study revealed that there is a significant positive relationship between neuroticism and non-vigilant decision styles. As neuroticism is related to maladaptive behaviour (Browne & Ekstrand, 1982) it is found in the present study that students with neuroticism dimension of personality tend to adopt all kinds of non-vigilant decision making styles (Maladaptive coping styles) in their decisions.

Since neuroticism is associated with arousability of Autonomous Nervous System (Eysenck, 1975a) during conflicting situations, students with neuroticism tendencies develop high emotional arousal and the obtained result proves that they overreact to such situations. Because of anxiety characteristic the individuals experience difficulties in assimilation of information (Mc Raynolds, 1976) they believe that they do not have control over the environment (Watson, 1967) and consider the situation in terms of loss (Wine, 1971).

Probably this would make the students to worry regardless of presence of threat (Mc Crae Robert,1990) and perceive relatively low level of confidence. So in such situations they experience panic and rely on hastily contrived solutions or sometimes try to avoid making decisions by putting the decisions off (procrastination) or by shifting the responsibility of taking decision onto someone else (Buck passing) or by justifying the least objectionable alternative (Rationalisation) and escape from decision situation. Experiencing much negative affect (Eysenck and Calvo, 1992) those who are high in neuroticism do not involve in decision making activities and are always at the mercy of the chance outcomes.

A negative correlation between neuroticism and decision self esteem obtained in the present study indicates that neuroticism tendency go along with low decision self esteem. The illusory confidence (Raymond,1990) and conformity characteristics (Brown, 1990) of neuroticism dimension may contribute to low decision self-esteem.

The result that neuroticism significantly correlates with all kinds of non-vigilant decision making styles and also with low decision self esteem leads to the conclusion that mediated by low decision self esteem, students with neuroticism dimension of personality tend to be non-vigilant in their decision. Therefore enhancing the decision self esteem of the students with neuroticism tendency in the domain of decision making skills (decision self esteem) would make them vigilant decision makers.

It is found in the present study that there is a significant negative correlation between psychoticism and vigilant decision making style. That is students with psychoticism dimension of personality are not making vigilant decisions. Studies reveal that psychoticism tendency is associated with little purpose in life (Pearson Paul, *et. al.,* 1989). So students with psychoticism tendency may not be clear in their objectives. Also psychoticism is characterised by solitary and engaged in little personal interaction (Eysenck,1975b). Consequently they may be short of information and even touch with reality. Hence students with psychoticism tendency can neither generate many alternatives, nor evaluate them (in light of their objectives) realistically. So they are not vigilant in their decision.

The present study also revealed a negative correlation between psychoticism and achievement motivation. Probably mediated by poor achievement motivation the students with psychoticism dimension of personality may not be vigilant in their decisions.

Demographic variables like the course of study and birth order are found to influence students decision making styles. Professional course students and first borns have more rationalising tendency than the rest of respective population. Here it is not clear whether studying professional course or the first birth order or both leads to rationalising decision styles among the students. Because, despite the methodological techniques, two important extraneous variables, left counter balanced are assumed to confound this result. Firstly, it so happened that most professional course students participated in the study were first borns and secondly there were not equal number of subjects in each birth order groups. Future researches counter balancing these variables would bring more light into this fact.

CONCLUSIONS

1. Decision making self-esteem positively correlates with vigilant decision making style and negatively correlates with non-vigilant styles.
2. Extraversion has a significant positive correlation with vigilant decision style and a significant negative correlation with procrastination and buck passing styles.
3. Neuroticism has a significant positive correlation with all non-vigilant decision styles.
4. Psychoticism has a significant negative correlation with vigilant decision style and a significant positive correlation with procrastination style.
5. Psychoticism has significant negative correlation with achievement motivation.
6. Achievement motivation has significant positve correlation with vigilant decision style.
7. Males have higher decision making self-esteem than females.
8. Professional course students have higher Neuroticism tendency and more often adopt rationalisation style when compared to Non-Professional Course students.
9. Non-Professional course students have higher psychoticism tendency and higher achievement motivation than Professional Course students.
10. First borns more often adopt Rationalisation style when compared to the second and later borns.

SUGGESTIONS FOR FURTHER RESEARCH

1. The present study can be replicated with university students of different places at the national level or international level.
2. The study can be replicated with the sample of students who just enter into college studies.
3. The study can be conducted with a larger sample.
4. Unless a correlation research, attempts can be made to study the cause and effect relationships between personality characteristics and decision making styles.
5. Self-efficacy, time pressure etc., can be studied in relation to conflict model of decision making.
6. Rural and Urban differences and Socio-economic status can also be studied with regard to decision making styles.
7. A review of literature on Self-esteem shows that first borns have more self-esteem than later borns. This result holds good only for males but not for females (Bolagi K. Yusuff, 1990). Further researches in this regard i.e. on sex categories may be conducted to see whether this relationship also holds for decision making self-esteem.
8. As the birth order is found to influence decision making styles (i.e. Rationalisation), further studies can be conducted with equal number of subjects in the three levels of birth order groups.
9. Contemporary psychologists realize the important influence of situational determinants in predicting human behaviour (e.g. Eysenck, 1967; Wallach and Leggett, 1972). So, the present study can be conducted in relation to other situational

determinants like achievement arousal conditions etc.

10. Studies reveal that consistency across situation and stability over time tend to be greater for behaviours associated with intelligence and cognitive process (e.g. Bloom, 1964; Gardner & Long, 1960; Kogan & Moss, 1962; Moss & Kogan, 1961). As decision making is a cognitive process, these variables may be studied in relation to decision making styles.

11. When extraversion correlates with vigilance, it does not correlate with decision self esteem one of the important correlates of vigilance. That is, extraversion leads to Vigilant decision via decision self esteem is not confirmed. But it was confirmed in the case of neuroticism. This is a gap in our knowledge which may be studied in future researches.

Appendix - I

ANNAMALAI UNIVERSITY DEPARTMENT OF PSYCHOLOGY

This study is on Decision Making styles and Personality make-up of individuals. In this connection I would be grateful if you can extend your co-operation by furnishing the required information. Kindly furnish answers to every question. Strict confidentiality of information is assured and further it is promised that this information would be used only for Research purposes.

Yours truly,

D. Amalor.

Dr. V. Suresh, M.A., M. Phil., Ph.D.
Professor & Head
Psychology Wing
Directorate of Distance Education
Annamalai University
(Guide)

Please furnish the following information :

1. Name :
2. Sex :
3. Age :
4. Course of Study :
5. Birth Order :

QUESTIONNAIRE – I

Instruction:

Please answer each question by putting a circle around the 'Yes' or the 'No' following each question. There are no right or wrong answers and no trick questions. Work quickly and do not think too long about the exact meaning of the questions.

1. Does your mood often go up and down? Yes/No
2. Do you take much notice of what people think? Yes/No
3. Are you a talkative person? Yes/No
4. If you say you will do something, do you always keep your promise no matter how inconvenient it might be? Yes/No
5. Do you ever feel 'just miserable' for no reason? Yes/No
6. Would being in debt worry you? Yes/No
7. Are you rather lively? Yes/No
8. Were you ever greedy by helping yourself to more than your share of anything? Yes/No
9. Are you an irritable person? Yes/No
10. Would you take drugs, which may have strange, or dangerous effects? Yes/No
11. Do you enjoy meeting new people? Yes/No
12. Have you ever blamed someone for doing something you knew was really your fault? Yes/No
13. Are your feelings easily hurt? Yes/No

14. Do you prefer to go your own way rather than act by the rules? Yes/No
15. Can you usually let yourself go and enjoy yourself at a lively party? Yes/No
16. Are all your habits good and desirable ones? Yes/No
17. Do you often feel 'fed-up'? Yes/No
18. Do good manners and cleanliness matter much to you? Yes/No
19. Do you usually take the initiative in making new friends? Yes/No
20. Have you ever taken anything (even a pin or button) that belonged to someone else? Yes/No
21. Would you call yourself a nervous person? Yes/No
22. Do you think marriage is old fashioned and should be done away with? Yes/No
23. Can you easily get some life into a rather dully party? Yes/No
24. Have you ever broken or lost something belonging to someone else? Yes/No
25. Are you a worrier? Yes/No
26. Do you enjoy co-operating with others? Yes/No
27. Do you tend to keep in the background on social occasions? Yes/No
28. Does it worry you if know there are mistakes in your work? Yes/No
29. Have you ever said anything bad or nasty about anyone? Yes/No

30. Would you call yourself tense or 'highly-strung'? Yes/No

31. Do you think people spend too much time safeguarding their future with savings and insurances? Yes/No

32. Do you like mixing with people? Yes/No

33. As a child were you ever cheeky to your parents? Yes/No

34. Do you worry too long after an embarrassing experience? Yes/No

35. Do you try to not to be rude people? Yes/No

36. Do you like plenty of bustle and excitement around you? Yes/No

37. Have you ever cheated at a game? Yes/No

38. Do you suffer from being 'nervous'? Yes/No

39. Would you like other people to be afraid of you? Yes/No

40. Have you ever taken advantage of someone? Yes/No

41. Are you mostly quiet when you are with other people? Yes/No

42. Do you often feel lonely? Yes/No

43. Is it better to follow society's rules than go your own way? Yes/No

44. Do other people think of you as being very lively? Yes/No

45. Do you always practise what you preach? Yes/No

46. Are you often troubled about feelings of guilt? Yes/No

47. Do you sometime put off until tomorrow what you thought to do today? Yes/No

48. Can you get a party going? Yes/No

QUESTIONNAIRE-II

Instruction

Kindly read each of the following statements and it's three alternative responses. Then you have to select one most suitable response out of them and tick (✓) against the selected response.

For example:

I like to

(a) do light works

(b) repair the broken articles or things

(c) collect information about new inventions.

In the above example, suppose out of the responses (a), (b), and (c) you prefer (b) as the most suitable response, tick (✓) against (b). Similarly, you have to select the most suitable answer for every statement. Kindly give the responses for all the statements.

1. I believe that after 10 years, I will...

   (a) Earn a lot of money

   (b) Achieve my desired vocation

   (c) Be known as a renowned person in my area of work.

2. I would like to study those subjects in which ...

   (a) less labour is needed

(b) higher probability of success is definite

(c) generally difficulty is felt

3. I think to get better marks in examination depends upon...

(a) teacher's good will

(b) encouragement of parents and relatives

(c) hard labour

4. I feel happy when I ...

(a) remain busy with my friends

(b) get an opportunity of leadership

(c) get an opportunity to help any person.

5. In future I will like to adopt an occupation which...

(a) requires least responsibility

(b) provide the opportunity to help others.

(c) contain more opportunities of promotion.

6. When I start my work, I...

(a) leave it when I feel bored.

(b) leave it when it seems to be difficult.

(c) never leave it incomplete.

7. At my leisure I like to...

(a) gossip with my friends

(b) play with my class-mates

(c) extend my co-operation in social welfare activities.

8. I like to ...

(a) do light work

(b) repair the broken articles/things

(c) collect information about new inventions.

9. If I were an engineer, I would like to...

(a) earn money

(b) construct beautifully designed buildings

(c) be involved in the researches related to new technologies

10. Before starting any work, I

(a) prepare its plan

(b) discuss it with the experienced person

(c) perceive the probable problems and find out their solutions

11. I study at home lest...

(a) my parents will rebuke me

(b) I will be blamed for being unsuccessful in the examination

(c) I will fail in the examination.

12. I wish that in future I,

(a) should be known as politician

(b) should be able to help others.

(c) should become a successful and renowned social worker

13. I like to become rich by...

(a) doing any type of work

(b) winning lottery

(c) earning money through hard work

14. At leisure I like to read....
    (a) the detective (Jasusi) novels and film magazine
    (b) comics
    (c) knowledgeable books
15. I wish to be recognised in the society by...
    (a) leading religious functions.
    (b) Serving the patients
    (c) By doing something extraordinary.
16. I will feel very happy if...
    (a) I get an opportunity to guide and supervise the work of others.
    (b) People honour my ability and seek my help.
    (c) People accept my guidance with full faith and confidence.
17. I pay respect to those who...
    (a) leave their work incomplete.
    (b) change their goal on getting other work.
    (c) continue their efforts till the goal is achieved
18. When the light suddenly goes at study time, I...
    (a) feel happy of being free from study
    (b) feel irritated
    (c) complete my work with the light or candle/ kerosene lamp.
19. If I were a doctor, I would like to...
    (a) earn money
    (b) provide free medicines to the patients
    (c) be a successful surgeon.

20. I like to do such work by which I may be counted among the ...
    (a) rich people
    (b) respectable persons of the society
    (c) famous people of the country
21. I like to utilize my knowledge in the tasks through which I may get...
    (a) money
    (b) fame
    (c) self satisfaction.
22. According to my opinion, the most important achievement of life is...
    (a) happy family life.
    (b) participation in the social welfare
    (c) to work for the fulfillment of the needs of the country.
23. I usually think to ....
    (a) make as many friends as I could
    (b) help the poor and needy person
    (c) remove the social evils and mischief.
24. When I take up my work, I try to...
    (a) complete it within due course of time
    (b) do it neatly and cleanly
    (c) do it better than others
25. I like to make my friends with those persons who...
    (a) believe that success depends upon fate and God

(b) start their work without any hesitation

(c) keep the caliber to lead their work successfully.

26. When I fail to follow a lesson, then...

(a) I leave that lesson

(b) I take help from others to understand that lesson

(c) I try again and again to follow that lesson.

27. I feel happy to...

(a) see others in trouble

(b) see others happy

(c) assist others

28. I start any work with the aim to complete...

(a) as soon as possible

(b) an organised manner

(c) with full competence

29. In writing articles, I give importance to

(a) the length of the article

(b) hand-writing

(c) language and thought

30. I like to be involved in such work...

(a) which will give me an opportunity to achieve some extra competence

(b) through which I may get an opportunity to know my weaknesses and improve them.

(c) In which chances of success are rare.

31. I feel proud of those friends who...
    (a) achieve pass marks in examination
    (b) provide help to weaker students
    (c) get brilliant success in examination
32. I feel the most important work in life is to...
    (a) earn money
    (b) motivate others for better work
    (c) achieve the excellent competence in work.
33. I like those people who...
    (a) are honest towards their job
    (b) are conscious towards their job
    (c) do their job with full devotion and honesty.
34. I often desire to
    (a) be recognised as a leader.
    (b) achieve the ability to do something meaningful
    (c) serve the patients
35. When I do any work, I like to start it...
    (a) without any pre-thinking
    (b) systematically
    (c) with full efficacy
36. I feel the progress of an occupation depends on ....
    (a) sources of income
    (b) contact with the influential person
    (c) hard labour

37. I respect those persons who...
    (a) work because they feel it is their duty
    (b) work to keep them busy
    (c) indulge themselves in the work with full devotion and competence.
38. On visualising an injured person in an accident, I feel ...
    (a) people should help him.
    (b) it is enough to inform the police
    (c) it is my duty to hospitalize him as soon as possible.
39. I like to work for...
    (a) myself
    (b) others
    (c) the nation.
40. I feel sad when...
    (a) I am punished by the teacher
    (b) my work is compared with others
    (c) I failed to achieve my goal.

QUESTIONNAIRE-III

Instruction

People differ in how comfortable they feel about making decisions. Please indicate how you feel about making decisions by ticking (✓) the response which is most applicable to you.

	True for me	some times	Not true
When making decisions,			
1. I feel confident about my ability to make decisions.	( )	( )	( )
2. I feel inferior to most people in making decisions.	( )	( )	( )
3. I think I am a good decision maker.			
4. I feel so discouraged that I give up trying to make decisions.	( )	( )	( )
5. The decision I make turn out well.	( )	( )	( )
6. It is easy for other people to convince me that their decision rather than mine is the correct one.	( )	( )	( )

QUESTIONNAIRE - IV

Instruction:

People differ in the way they go about making decisions. Please indicate how you make decisions by ticking (✓) for each question the response which best fits your usual style.

	True for me	some times	Not true
When making decisions:			
1. I feel as if I am under tremendous time pressure.	( )	( )	( )
2. I feel better about choosing if I can convince myself that the decision is not all that important.	( )	( )	( )
3. I like to consider all the alternatives.	( )	( )	( )
4. When I have a decision to make I try not to think about it.	( )	( )	( )

	True for me	some times	Not true
5. I prefer to leave decisions to others.	( )	( )	( )
6. Whenever I get upset by having to make decision I choose on the spur of the moment.	( )	( )	( )
7. I try to find out the disadvantage of all the alternatives.	( )	( )	( )
8. I am inclined to blame others when decisions turn out badly.	( )	( )	( )
9. I waste a lot of time on trivial matters.	( )	( )	( )
10. I feel uncomfortable about making decisions.	( )	( )	( )
11. I considered how to carry out decisions.	( )	( )	( )
12. Even after I have made a decision I delay acting up on it.	( )	( )	( )
13. After making a decision, I am inclined to undervalue the worth of the alternatives I did not choose.	( )	( )	( )
14. When making a decision I like to collect lot of information.	( )	( )	( )
15. I avoid making decisions.	( )	( )	( )
16. I only want to hear information about my preferred alternative.	( )	( )	( )
17. When I have to make decision, I wait a long time before starting to think about it.	( )	( )	( )
18. I don't like to take responsibility for making decisions.	( )	( )	( )
19. I try to be clear about my objectives before choosing.	( )	( )	( )
20. I forget or overlook important information about choice alternatives.	( )	( )	( )

	True for me	some times	Not true
21. The possibility that some small thing might go wrong cause me to swing abruptly in my preference.	( )	( )	( )
22. If a decision can be made by me or another person I let the other person make it.	( )	( )	( )
23. Whenever I face a difficult decision, I feel pessimistic about finding a good solution.	( )	( )	( )
24. I take a lot of care before choosing.	( )	( )	( )
25. I choose on the basis of some small thing.	( )	( )	( )
26. I don't make decision unless I really have to.	( )	( )	( )
27. I delay making decisions until it is too late.	( )	( )	( )
28. I prefer that people who are better informed decide for me.	( )	( )	( )
29. After a decision is made I spend a lot of time convincing myself it was correct.	( )	( )	( )
30. I put off making decisions.	( )	( )	( )
31. I can't think straight if I have to make decision in a hurry.	( )	( )	( )

Bibliography

Adanijo, I.B. and Adenekan Oyefeso (1986). Developing a self report scale of self esteem. Paper presented in the Rid Annual Conference of Nigerian Psychological Association, Nuskka.

Adenekan Oyefeso and Pius A.Baiyere (1990). Self-esteem and Family type as predictors of Affiliantiveness among Nigerian adolescents, *Asian Journal of Psychology and Education,* Vol. 23, No. 1-2, pp. 30-35.

Ajith K. Dalal and Anitha Sethi (1988). An attributional Study of High and low need Achievers in India: *Journal of Social Psychology*, Vol. 128, No. 1, pp. 55-64.

Anderson J.R. (1985). *Cognitive Psychology and its Implications*, 2nd ed. New York: W.H. Freeman.

Aronson (1980). Counseling and personal decision: Theory and Researches on short term helping Relationships. In I.L. Janis (Ed.) *New Haven*, Yale University Press.

Asghar Ali (1989). A comparative study of achievement Motivation, creativity and personality need of destitute boys and girls, *Indian Psychological Review,* Vol. 34, Nos. 8, 9, 10 pp. 21-25.

Atkins (1988). Decision making in curriculum conferences: A study of convergence of optimism. *Journal of curriculum studies*. Vol. 22, No. 4 pp. 343-360.

Atkinson J.W. and Litwin G.H. (1960). Achievement motive and test anxiety conceived as a motive to approach Success and to avoid Failure. *Journal of Abnormal Social Psychology*, 60; pp. 52-63.

Atkinson, J.W. (1957). Motivational determinants of risk-taking behaviour. *Psychological Review*, 64, pp. 359-372.

Atkinson, J.W. (1978). *Introduction to Motivation*, John W. Atkinson and David Birch; D. Van Nostrand company NY.

Atkinson, J.W. and Feather, N.T. (1966). *A Theory of Achievement Motivation*, Huntington N.Y. Krieger.

Bales, R.F. (1950). Interaction process analysis; a method for the study of small groups. Cambridge, Mass: Addison-Wesley.

Barief, M.L. and Lusk, E.J. (1977). Cognitive and personality tests for the design of Management information systems. *Management Science*, April, pp. 820-29.

Barry , H; Bacon, M.K. and Child, I.L. (1957). A cross cultural survey of some sex differences in socialisation. *Journal of Abnormal and Social Psychology.* 55. pp. 327-32.

Bem, D.J., Wallach, M.H. and Kogan, N (1965). Group decision making under risk of aversive consequences, *Journal of Personality and Social Psychology*, 1, pp. 453-60.

Berger-cross, V., Kahn, M.W., and Weare, C.R. (1983). The role of anxiety in career decision making liberal arts students. *Journal of Vocational Behaviour*, 22, pp. 312-33.

Berkowitz, L and R.M. Lundy (1957). Personality characteristics related to susceptibility to influence by peers or authority figures. *Journal of Personality,* Vol. 25, pp. 306-16.

Beswick, G. (1981). Decision making styles and personality. Unpublished manuscript, The Flinders University of South Australia. School of Social Sciences.

Biondo and Mac Donald (1971). Counseling and personal decision: Theory and Researches on short term helping Relationships. In I.L. Janis (Ed.) *New Haven*. Yale University Press.

Birch, H.G (1945). The relation of previous experience to insightful problem solving. *Journal of Comp. Psychol*. Vol. 38, pp. 367-83.

Blaylock, B.K. and Rees, L.P. (1984). Cognitive styles and the usefulness of information. *Decision Science*. Vol. 15, pp. 74-91.

Block (1976). Personality. In Paul R. Abramson (ed.).Holt Rinehart and Winston, New York, 1980

Bloom (1964). Personality and Assessment. In Walter Mischel (Ed.) New York Wiely. 1968.

Bolaji, K.Yusuff (1990). Comparative Analysis of birth order and Self- esteem among University Athletes, *Asian Journal of Psychology and Education*, Vol. 23, Nos. 1-2, pp. 22-29.

Bolgar Nial (1990). Coping as a personality process; A prospective study. *Journal of personality and Social Psychology,* (Sep) Vol 59(3), pp. 525-37.

Bond, M (1981). An investigation of the relationships between selected personality traits and the stress inducing concerns, and the coping mechanisms inherent in decision making. Unpublished manuscript. The Flinders University of south Australia, School of Social Sciences.

Broadhurst, P.L. (1959). The interatction of task difficulty and motivation. The Yerkes-Dodson Law Reviewed. *Acta Psychologica*, 16, pp. 32-38

Brown, G.W, Andrews, B, Bifulco, A. and veiel, H. (1990). Selfesteem and Depression: Measurement issues and prediction of onset. *Social Phsychiatry and Psychiatric Epidemology*, Vol. 25(4), pp. 200-209.

Burnett, P.C. Mann, L. Beswic, G. (1989). Validation of the Flinders Decision making Questionnaire on course decision making by students. *Australian Psychologist.* Vol. 24(2), pp. 285-292.

Cairns, E.D. M.C. Whirter, Liz Duffy Ursulla and Barry Robert. (1990). The stability and situational effets. *Personality and Individual Differences*, Vol. 11(9), pp. 937-44.

Campbell, R. (1981). Individual difference and decision making. An analysis using the conflict model. Unpublished manuscript. The Flinders University of South Australia, School of Social Sciences.

Carlson (1971, 1977). Personality. In Paul R. Abramson (ed.). Holt Rinehart and Winston. New York, 1980

Chaudhary Nirmala (1972). The relationships between n Ach and Anxiety Intelligence, Sex, Social class and vocational aspirants, *Indian Psychological Abstracts,* Vol. 1, No. 3 May, June p. 153.

Cheryl Ormond *et. al.* (1991). A metacognitive analysis of decision making in adolescence. *Journal of Adolescence,* 14, pp. 275-291.

Coleman Campbell and Hobson MC. Partland (1966). Counseling and personal decision: Theory and Researches on short term helping Relationships. In I.L. Janis (Ed.), *New Haven*, Yale University Press.

Coles, M. (1971). Personality and habituation of the orienting reaction: Tonic and response measure of electrodermal energy, *Psychophysiology*, 8, pp. 54-63.

Coopersmith, S. (1967). *The antecedents of self-esteem.* San Francisco: W.H. Freeman & Co.

Coopersmith, S. (1978). *Psychology of adjustment.* In Atwater (Ed.), New Jersey, Printice Hall inc.

Crandall, V.C. (1969). Sex difference in expectancies of intellectual and academic reinforcement. In C.P. Smith (Ed.) *Achievement-related motives in children*, NY: Russell Sage Foundation.

Crowmwell R.L. (1963). A social learning approach to mental retardation. *Hand book of mental deficiency*, NY : Mc.Graw. Hill.

Crowne, D.P. and Bonnie R. Stickland (1961)The conditioning of verbal behaviour as a function of the need for social approval. *J. Abnormal. Soc. Psychol*, Vol. 63, 395-401.

Davis Donald, L. Grove Stephen, J. and Knowels Partricia, A. (1990), An experimental application of personality type as an analogue for decision-making style. *Psychological Reports*, Vol. 66(1), 167-75.

De. B and Priya Shampoo (1972). Some personal and academic correlates of n Ach, *Indian Psychological Abstracts*, Vol. 1, No. 3, May-June, p. 153.

Deaux *et. al.* (1975). Skill versus Luck; Field and Laboratory studies of male and female references. *Journal of Personality and Social Psychology*, 32, pp. 629-36.

Dember, W.N. (1964). Birth order and need affiliation. *Journal of abnormal and social psychology*, Vol. 68, pp. 555-57

Dermer, J.D. (1973). Cognitive characteristic and the perceived importance of information. *Accounting Review*, 48, pp. 511-19.

Dinklage (1966). Psychology of adjustment. In Atwater, E (Ed.) Prentice Hall Inc. New Jersey, 1983.

Distefano, Pryor and Smith (1987). Comparisons of normal adolescents, Psychiatric patients and adults on internal-external control. *Jrl. of Clinical Psychology*, 27, 343-45.

Dittes (1959). Counseling and personal decision: Theory and Researches on short term helping Relationships. In I.L. Janis (Ed.), *New Haven*, Yale University Press.

Donn Byrne (1966). *Introduction to personality: Research, Theory and Applications*: Donn Byrne (2nd Ed.) Prentice Hall, New Jersey, 1974.

Driscoll J.M. and Lanzetta J.T. (1964). Effects of problem uncertainty and prior arousal as predecisional information search. *Psychological Reports*, 14, pp. 975-88.

Duffy, E. (1957). The Psychological significance of the concept of "arousal" or "activation". *Psychol. Rev.* 1959, 64, 265-275.

Edwards (1954). *Personality: Motivation and achievement.* John W Atkinson and Joel O. Raynor. Hemisphere Pub. Washington.

Edwards, A.L. (1953). Manual of the Edwards Personal Preference schedule, San Antonio, Texas: The Psychological Corporation.

Escalona, S.K. (1940). The effect of success and failure upon the level of aspiration and behaviour in manic-depressive psychoses. Univ. Iowa. *Stud. Child Welf*, 16, 199-302.

Etringer Bruce D. *et. al.* (1990). The influence of sexual orientation on career decision making; A Research note. *Journal of Homosexuality*, Vol. 19 (4), pp. 103-11.

Eysenck S.B.G., Eysenck, H.J. and Paul Barrett (1985). A revised version of the Psychoticism Scale, *Journal of personality and individual difference,* Vol. 6 (1), pp. 21-29.

Eysenck, H.J. and Eysenck S.B.G. (1976). *Psychoticism as a dimension of personality*, London, Hodder and Stoughton.

Eysenck, H.J. (1973). *Eysenck on Extraversion*, N.Y. Wiley.

Eysenck, H.J. (1975 a). *Motivation and Emotion*, Phil Evans (Ed.) Billing & Sons Ltd., Worecester, London 1989, pp. 94-95.

Eysenck, H.J. Eysenck S.B.G. (1975). Mannual of Eysenck Personality Questionnaire. San Diego, CA: Ed ITS.

Eysenck, H.J. (1975b). Persnality: Strategies and issues: Robert M. Liebert and Mischel D. Spiegler (Ed.) *The Dorsery Press*. Home wood Illinois, 1978. 232-34.

Eysenck, M.W. and Calvo, M. (1992). Anxiety and performance: The processing effiecency theory. *Cognition and Emotion*, Vol. 6, pp. 409-34.

Eysenck, H.J. (1967). *The Biological Basis of Personality*, Springfield, Illinois. Thomas.

Eysenck, H.J. and Eysenck, S.B.G. (1963). On the dual nature of extraversion. *British Journal of Social and Clinical Psychology*, Vol. 2, pp. 46-55.

Fatmi, S, Bakhteyar (1990). Family structure variables and achievement motivation among high school students. *Indian Journal of Applied Psychology,* Vol. 27(1), pp. 25-28.

Feather, N. and Mann, L. (1982). Masculinity, depression and self-esteem and their relationship to the DMQ subscales. Unpublished manuscript. The Flinders university of South Australia, School of Social Sciences.

Festinger, L. (1942). A Theoretical interpretation of shifts in level of aspiration. *Psychol. Rev.* 49, pp. 235-50.

Fishbein, M. and Ajzen, L. (1975). *Belief, Attitude, Intention and Behaviour*; London: Addison-Wesley.

Fishman Claire (1965). Need for approval and the expression of agression under varying conditions of frustration. *J. Per. Soc. Psychol.* 2, pp. 809-16

Flavell, J. and Wellman, H.L. (1977). Metamemory. In perspectives on the development of memory and cognition. R.Kail and Kagen (Eds.) Hillsdale, N.J. Lawrence, Erlbaum Associates.

Fredrickson James, W. (1986). Effects of decision motive and organisational performance level on strategic decision process. *American Psychological Abstract,* Vol. 75(5), pp. 13799-13809.

French and Thomas (1958): The relation of achievement motivation to problem-solving effectiveness. *Journal of abnormal and Social Psychology*, 56, 45-48.

Gardner and Long (1960). Personality and Assessment. In Walter Mischel (Ed.), New York, Wiley 1968.

Garg K. (1981):Self-esteem and academic achievement among Adolescents, *Progress of Education*, 55(6) pp. 156-59.

Gelatt H.B., Barbara Varenhorst, Richard Carey and Corden P.Miller (1973). *Decision and Outcomes: A leader's Guide. College Entrance Examination Board*, New York, 1973, pp. 8-9.

Gelatt, H.B. (1962). Decision making. A conceptual Frame of reference for counseling, *Jrl. of counseling psychology*, 9, pp. 240-45.

George, E.T.and Abraham, P.A. (1975). Order of birth and some personality traits, Adjustment and Achievement of secondary School Pupils. *Indian Psychological Abstract,* Vol. 7.

Ghani, J. and Lusk, E.J. (1982). Human information processing research: Its MIS design on sequences. *Human Systems Management*, March, pp. 32-40.

Gokulnathan, P.P. (1975). *Indian Psychological Abstracts,* Vol. 7, p. 133.

Gordon, L.V. (1975). The measurement of Interpersonal values. Chicago, Ill. Science Research Association.

Govind Tiwari (1983). Risk taking tendencies as correlates of self esteem, asperiation and deviancy. *Bombay Psychologist,* Vol. 5 (1), pp. 29-35.

Graybill (1978). *Psychology of Adjustment*. In Atwater, E. (Ed.) Prentice Hall Inc., New Jersey, 1983.

Gurna Ernest, B and Balbon Mark,(1990). Self evaluation of physical attractiverness as a function of self esteem and defensiveness. *Journal of Social Behaviour and Personality*, Vol. 5 (6), pp. 575-80.

Hall Evelyn, G. (1990). The effect of performer gender, performer skill level and opponent gender on self confidence in a competitive situation. *Sex Roles*, (July), Vol. 23 (1-2), pp. 33-41.

Halsam, D. (1967). Individual difference in pain threshold and level of arousal. *British Journal of Psychology*, 58, pp. 139-42.

Harren, V.A. (1976). Assessment of career decision making. Iowa. City American College, Testing program.

Heaton Allen W. (1991). Person perception by introverts and extraverts under time pressure: Effects of need for closure. *Personality and social psychology Bulletin.* Vol. 17(2), pp. 161-65.

Heaven Patric, C. (1990). Religious values and personality dimensions. *Personality and individual differences*, Vol. 11 (9), pp. 953-56.

Hebb, D.O. (1955). Drives and the C.N.S. (Conceptual nervous system) *Psychol. Rev.*, 62, pp. 243-54.

Herek, G. Janis I.L.and Huth P. (1987). Decision making during international crisis: Is quality of process related to outcome? *Journal of Conflict Resolution,* 31, pp. 203-26.

Hilton, (1967). Difference in the behaviours of mothers towards first and later born children. *Journal of Personality and Social Psychology,* 7, pp. 202-90.

Holdstein, Goldstein and Bem (1971). Counseling and personal decision: Theory and Researches on short term helping Relationships. In I.L. Janis (Ed.), *New Haven*, Yale University Press.

Hollis, J.W. and Hollis, Lucile, V. (1969). *Personalising Information Process*, N.Y.: MacMillan.

Horner (1972). The motive to avoid success and changing aspirations of college women. In J.M. Bardwick (Ed.) *Reading: On Psychology of Women*, N.Y., Harper and Row.

Hunt Ramond G. *et. al.* (1989). Cognitive style and decision making. *Journal of Organisational behaviour and Human decision process* (2nd Ed.), Dec. Vol. 44 (3), pp. 436-53.

Hunt, E. and Lansman, M. (1975). Cognitive theory applied to individual differences. In *Hand Book of Learning and Cognitive Process*, Hillsdale, NJ. Lawrence Erlbaum.

Hyland, M.E ; Curtis, C and Mason, D. (1985). Fear of success motive and cognition. *Journal of Personality and Social Psychology*, 49, pp. 1669-77.

Irwin, F.W. and Smith W.A.S. (1956). Further tests of theories of decision in an expanded judgement' situation. *Journal of Experimental Psychology,* 52, pp. 345-48.

Isaacson, R.L.(1964). Relation between need achievement, test anxiety and curricular choices. *Journal of Abnormal and Social Psychology,* Vol. 68, pp. 447-52.

James C. Hansen, Richard R. Stevic and Richards W.Warner (1972). *Counselling Theory and Process*. Allyn and Bacon inc. Boston, 1977.

Janis and Mann (1977). Decision making; A psychological analysis of conflict, choice and commitment, N.Y., The Free Press.

Janis, I.L. and Field P.B. (1959). Sex differences and personality factors related to persuaasibility. In. C.I. Hovland, P.B. Field, H.Linton, E. Graham, A.R. Cohen, D.Rife, R.P. Abelson, G.S.Lesser and B.T. King. (Eds.) *Personality and Persuaasibility*, New Heaven, Conn. Yale.

Karim shamin F. (1990). Self concept: A cross cultural study on adolescents *Psychological studies*, Vol. 35 (2), pp. 118-23.

Keating, D.P. (1990). Adolescent thinking. In at the threshold. The developing adolescent. S. Feldman and G. Elliott (Eds). Cambridge Massachusetts: Harvard University Press.

Klein, G.S. (1971). *Psychoanalytic Theory: An Exploration of Essentials*, N.Y., Knopf.

Kogan and Moss (1962). *Personality and Assessment*. In Walter Mischel (Ed.), New York, Wiely 1968.

Kogan, N and Wallach, M.A. (1967). Risk-taking as a function of the situation, the person and the group. In Mandlor G, Mussen, P. Kogan N. and Wallach M.A. (Eds), *New Directions in psychology*, 11, N.Y., Halt Rinhart and Winston.

Kozelsski Jozet (1981). Psychological decision theory. *American Psychological Abstract*, Vol. 69(5), pp. 9599-9607.

Kureshi Afzal (1979). TAT study of motives of Hindu and Muslim Adolescents. *Indian Psychological Abstract*, Vol. 16, No. 3 September.

Larkin, J.H. *et. al.* (1980). Expert and Novice performance in solving physics problems. *Science*, 208, pp. 1335-45.

Lefcourt, H.M. (1966). Internal versus External control of reinforcement. A Review *Psychological Bulletin*, Vol. 65, pp. 206 -20

Lefcourt, H.M. (1972). Recent development in the study of locus of control. In *Progress in experimental Psychological Research*, N.Y. Academic Press.

Lesser, G.S. and Abelson,R.P. (1959). Personality ciorrelates of persuasibility in children. In I.L. Janis and C.I. Hovland (Eds.) *Personality and Persuasiblity. New Haven*, Yale University Press, pp. 187-206.

Leventhal, H. and S.I. Perloe (1962). A relationship between self esteem and persuasibility. *Journal of Abnormal and Social Psychology*, 64, pp. 385-88.

Lewin, K. (1938). Personality: Motivation and achievement. John W. Atkinson and Joel O. Raynor. Hemishpere Pub. Washington, 1978, p. 12.

Lewin, K. Tamara Dembo, I., Festinger and Pauline S.Sears (1944). Level of aspiration, In J. Mc. V. Hunt (Ed.) *Personality and the Behaviour Disorder*, Vol. 1, N.Y., Ronald.

Lindzey, G. and Aronson, E. (1954). *Hand Book of Social Psychology*. Cambridge Mass: Addison Wesley.

Linton (1945). Personality, Paul R. Abramson (Ed). Holt Rinehart and Winston, New York, 1980.

Litwin (1958). Motivation and Achievement. John W. Atkinson and Joel O. Raynor. Hemisphere Pub. Washington, 1978.

Long Barbara, H. and Ziller R.L. (1965). Dogmatism and predecisional information Search, *Journal of applied Psychology*, 9, pp. 376-78.

Lunneborg, P.W. (1978). Sex and career decision making styles. *Journal of Counselling Psychology*, 25, pp. 299-305.

Mac crimmon, K.R. (1973). Managerial decision making. In. J.W. Gurie (Ed.). Contemporary Management: Issues and View Points, Engle Wood Clifts, N.J. Prentice-Hall, pp. 445-95.

Mac Donald (1972). Counseling and personal decision: Theory and Researches on short term helping Relationships. In I.L. Janis (Ed.), *New Haven*, Yale University Press.

Maccoby, E.E. and Jacklin, C.N. (1974). *The Psychology of Sex Differences*. Standford, Calif: Standford.

Mahone, C. (1960). Fear of failure in unrealistic vocational aspiration". *Journal of Abnormal and Social Psychology*, 60, pp. 253-61.

Malmo, R.B. (1959). Activation: A neurophysiological dimension. *Psychological Review*, 66, pp. 367-386.

Mann, L (1982). Decision making Questionnaire Mannual; Leon Mann. The Flinders University of South Australia.

Mann, L., Beswick, G., Allouch, P. and Ivey, M. (1989). Decision workshops for the improvement of decision making skills and development, 67, pp. 478-81.

Mann, L., Harmoni, R.V., Power, C.N., Beswick, G., Ormond, C. (1988). Effectiveness of the GOFER course in decision making for the high school students. *Journal of behavioural decision making*, 1, pp. 159-168.

Mareck and Mettee (1972). Counseling and personal decision: Theory and Researches on short term helping Relationships. In I.L. Janis (Ed.) *New Haven*. Yale University Press.

Marlow, D. and D.P. Crowne (1961). Social desirability and response to percieved situational demands. *J. Consult. Psychol,* 25, pp. 109-115.

Marlowe (1962). Need for social approval and operant conditioning of meaningful verbal behaviour. *J.consult.psychol*, 26, pp. 79-83.

Marlowe,D.R.S. Beecher, J.B; Cock and A.N. Doob (1964). The approval motive, vicarious reinforcement and verbal conditioning. *Percept. Mot. Skills*, 19, pp. 523-30.

Mc Clelland, D.C. *et. al*: (1953). *The Achievement Motive*: N.Y., Appleton-Century-Crofts.

Mc. Rae. Robert, R. (1990). Controlling neuroticism in the measurement of stress. Advances in measuring life stress. *Stress medicine*, (July-Sept.), Vol. 6 (3), pp. 237-41. (Advancer in Meaning life stress).

Mc. Reynolds, P. (1976). Assimilation and anxiety: In M.zuckerman and C.D. Spielberger (Ed) Emotion and Anxiety: New concepts methods and application. Hills dale. N.J. Lawrence, Erlbaum, 1976.

Meador, B.D. and Rogers, C.R. (1973). Client centred therapy. In current Psychotherapies, R. Corsini (Ed.) Itasca, Illinois: F.E. Peacock Pub, inc.

Meena Sehgal (1984). Psychoticism, Reinforcement and vigilance. *Indian Journal of Psychology,* Vol. 59, No. 3-4 Sep-Dec. pp. 20-23.

Meese, J.L. Eccles-Parsons, J. Kaczala, C.M.; Croff, S.B. and Futterman, R. (1982). Sex difference in math achievement. Toward a model of academic choice, *Psychological Bulletin*, 91, pp. 324-48.

Mischel, W and Carole Gilligan (1964). Delay of gratification, motivation for the prohibited gratification and responses to temptation, *Journal of Abnormal and Social Psychology,* Vol. 69, pp. 411-17.

Monterio (1978). *Psychology of Adjustment.* In Atwater, E. (Ed.) Prentice Hall Inc., New Jersey, 1983.

Moore J. William; Jense Brian and Hauck William, E (1990). Decision making process of youth. *Adolescence,* Vol. 25 (99), pp. 583-92.

Moss and Kogan (1961). *Personality and Assessment.* In Walter Mischel (Ed.), New York, Wiely 1968.

Muecher, H. and H. Heckhausen (1962). Influence of mental activity and achievement motivation on skeletal muscles tonus, *Percept. Mot. Skills,* Vol. 14, pp. 217-18.

Mukherji, B.N. and Sinha, R. (1970). Achievement values and self-ideal discrepancies in college students, *Personality: An International Journal,* Vol. 1, pp. 275-301.

Mussen (1969). Personality. Paul R. Abramson (Ed). Holt Rinehart and Winston. New York 1980.

Myers and Mc. Caulley, (1985). Mannual. A guide to the development and use of the Myers-Briggs Type Indicator, Palo Alto, C.A. Counseling Psychology Press, p. 13.

Nair, P.R.K. (1986). A study of achievement motivation among officers of Business group in a Public Enterprises. *Indian Journal of Community Guidance and Service,* Vol. 3, No. 1 Jan.

Newell, A. and Simon, H.A. (1972). Human Problem Solving. Englewood Cliffs. N.J: Prentice-Hall.

Odel (1959). Counseling and Personal Decision: Theory and Researches on short-term helping Relationships. In I.L. Janis (Ed.), *New Haven.* Yale University Press.

Olof, Dahiback (1990). Personality and Risk taking. *Personality and individual differences*, Vol. 11 (12), pp. 1235-42.

Pearson Paul R. and Sheffield Brian,F(1989). Psychoticism and purpose in life. *Personality and Individual Differences*, 10(2), pp. 1321-22

Plante Thomas G. and Schwartz Garry, E (1990). Defensive and Repressive coping styles: Self presentation, leisure activities and assessment. *Journal of Research in Personality,* (June) Vol. 24(2), pp. 73-190.

Priyamvada Srivastava Ku. (1989). Decision making and Personality Traits, *Indian Psychological Review,* Vol. 34, No. 11-12, p. 1729.

Radford, M.H.B. Mann, L. and Kalucy, R.S. (1986). Psychiatric disturbance and decision making. *Australia and New Zealand Journal of Psychiatry*, 20, pp. 210-217.

Radford, M.H.B.(1982). An investigation into the relationship between self esteem and decision making. A conflict model approach. Unpublished manuscript. The Flinders University of South Australia.

Radformd, M.H.B.,Mann, L; Ohta,Y; and Nakane,Y; (1989). Individual decision making Behaviour and personality: A priliminary Study using a Japanese University Sample. *The Japanese Journal of Experimental Social Psychology*, Vol. 28 (2), pp. 115-22.

Rathi (1981). Locus of control and achievement motivation, *Perspectives in Psychological Researches*, Vol. 4, No. 2, pp. 17-20.

Ray, J.J. (1990). Some cross cultural explorations of the relationship between achievement motivation and anxiety. *Personality and individual differences,* Vol. 11 (1), pp. 91-93.

Raymond, Wolfe, N and Grosch James, W (1990). Personality correlates of confidence in one's decisions. *Journal of Personality*, Vol. 58 (3), pp. 515-34.

Raynor, J.O. (1970). Relationship between achievement related motives, future orientation and academic performance. *Journal of Personality and Social Psychology*, 15, pp. 28-33.

Revelle *et. al.* (1976). Introversion/Extraversion, time, stress and Caffeine: the effect of verbal performance. *Science,* 192, pp. 149-50.

Richter Fderick, P. and Tosvold, D. (1980). Effects of students participation in classroom decision making attitudes, peer interactions, motivation and learning. *Journal of Applied Psychology,* Vol. 65(1), pp. 74-80.

Rim, Y. (1963). Risk-taking and need for achievement. *Acta Psychologica*, 21, pp. 108-15.

Ritchie and Phares (1969). Counseling and personal decision: Theory and Researches on short term helping Relationships. In I.L. Janis (Ed.), *New Haven,* Yale University Press.

Rokeach Milton and Barrow Frank (1960-1963). Scientific Creativity. Its recognition and development. *Adminstrative Science Quarterly,* June 1969, pp. 260-71.

Rosen, B.C. (1961). Family structure and achievement motivation. *Amer. Sociol. Rev.* 26, pp. 574-85.

Rosenberg, M. (1965). Society and the adlescent self image. Princeton, New Jersey: Princeton University Press.

Rotter, J.B. (1954). Personality: Motivation and achievement. In John W. Atkinson and Joel O. Raynor. Hemishpere Pub. Washington, 1978, p. 12.

Rotter, J.B. (1966). Generalised expectancies for Internal versus External control of reinforcement. *Psychological Monographs,* 80, No. 1 (Whole No. 609), pp. 1-28.

Rudin, S.A. (1964, 1965). What price glory? Psychosomatic death rates and motivation in 17 countries. *Acta Psychologica*. 23, p. 107.

Sampson E.A. *et. al.* (1967). An examination of the relationship between ordinal positions, Personality and Conformity. *Journal of Personality and Social Psychology,* 5, pp. 398-407.

Sampson, E.E.(1962). Birth order, need achievement and conformity. *Journal of Abnormal and Social Psychology,* Vol. 64, pp. 155-59.

Samual, W. (1980). Mood and personality correlates of IQ by race and sex of subject. *Journal of Personality and Social Psychology*, 38, pp. 1993-1004.

Samuel, W. Soto, D. Parks, M. Ngissah, P. and Jones, B. (1976). Motivation, Race, Social class and IQ. *Journal of Educational Psychology,* 68, pp. 273-85.

Sarason, I.G. (1957). Test anxiety, general anxiety and intellectual performance, *Journal of Consulting Psychology,* 21, pp. 435-90.

Sarason, I.G. (1975). Test anxiety, attention and the general problem of anxiety, In. C.D. Spielberger and I.G. Sarason (Ed). Stress and anxiety, NY. Wiley.

Schachter, S (1964a). Birth order and sociometric choice. *Journal of Abnormal and Social Psychology.*Vol. 68, pp. 453-56.

Sears, R.R. Msccoby, E and Levin, H. (1957). *Patterns of child Rearing*. Evanson, I.L. Row. Peterson.

Seeman, M. and Evans, J.W. (1963). Alienation and learning in a hospital situation. *American Sociological Review*, 27, pp. 772-783.

Shah Beena (1986). Mannual of Achievement motivation Scale (AMS) Shah Beena; Agra Psychological Research Cell, Agra.

Sharma, K.L. (1972). A study of achievement abasement need pattern in Indian personality. *Indian psychological Abstracts* Vol. (1), No. 3 May-June, p. 166.

Shrauger, J.S. and Rosenberg, S.E. (1970). Self esteem and the effect of success and failure feedback on performance. *Journal of Personality*, 38, pp. 104-417.

Simon H.A. and Paige, J.M. (1966). Cognitive process in solving algebra word problems. In B. Kleinmuntz (Ed.), *Problems Solving*, N.Y. John Wiley.

Singh S.V.V. (1978). Some Correlates of Psychoticism. *Indian Psychological Abstract*, Vol. 20 (4).

Slade, L. Allen and Rush Michael C (1991). Achievement Motivation and the dynamics of task difficulty choices. *Journal of Personality and Social Psychology*, Vol. 60(1), pp. 165-72.

Smith Barry D. *et. al.* (1990). Regression and criterion measure of habituation: A comparative analysis in extraverts and introverts. *Journal of Research in Personality,* 1990 (June) Vol. 24 (2), pp. 123-32.

Spence, J.T. and Spence, K.M. (1966). The motivational components of manifest anxiety. Drive and Drive Stimuli. In C.D. Spielberger (Ed.) *Anxiety and Behaviour*, N.Y., Academic.

Stein. A.H. and Bailey, M.M. (1973). The Socialisation of achievement orientation in female. *Psychological Bulletin,* 80, pp. 345- 366.

Stickland Bonnie, R and D.P. Crowne (1962). Conformity under conditions of simulated group pressure as a function of the need for social approval. *J. Soc. Psy,* 58, pp. 171-81.

Suinn, R.M. (1965). Anxiety and Intellectual performance: A partial failure to replicate. *Journal. of Consulting Psychology*, 29, p. 81.

Svenson, D A. Edland and P. Slovic (1990). Choices and judgments of completely described decision alternatives under time pressure. *Acta psychologica*, 75, pp. 153-169.

Tarrier Nichols, Becket Richard, Harwood Susan and Ahmed, Yasmin (1989). Comparison of a morbidly Jealous and a normal female population on the Eysenck Personality Questionnaire (EPQ). Personality and Individual differences, Vol. 10(12), pp. 1327-28.

Tashakkori Abbas; Thompson Vaide D, wade Joel and Velente Ernest (1990). Structure and stability of self esteem in late teens. Personality and individucal differences, Vol. 11(9), pp. 885-93.

Taylor, R.N. (1975). Age and Experience as determinants of managerial information processing and decision making performance. *Academy of management Journal,* 18, pp. 74-81.

Taylor, R.N. and Dunnett, M.D. (1974). Relative contribution of decision maker attributes for decision making process. *Organisational behaviour and human behaviour,* 12, 286-98.

Terry George (1972). *Principles of Management* (6th ed.) Richard D Irwin, Inc. Irwin Dargey Ltd.

Thamson Elzo (1990). A comparison between the achievement motivation of male and female school children in the Preotria and Witwatersand erea, South Africa, *Journal of Psychology,* Vol. 20(2), pp. 63-69.

Thanick Jozet and Stephen Vendel (1983). Indecision of Basic school Pupils at their vocational choice. *American Psychological Abstract,* Vol. 69(1), pp. 2000-11.

Thibaut, J.W. and Kelley, H.H. (1959). *The Social Psychology of Groups*, N.Y.: Wiley.

Tolman (1955). *Personality: Motivction and Achievement*, John W. Atkinson and Joel O. Raynor. Hemisphere Pub., Washington, 1978, p. 12.

Tresemer, D. (1976, 1877). *Fear of Success*. N.Y. Plenum Press.

Tversky, A. and Kahneman, D. (1974). Judgement under Uncertainty: Herustics and Biases. *Science,* Vol. 185, pp. 1124-31.

Veroff *et. al.* (1960). The use of Thematic apperception to assess motivation in a nation-wide interview study. *Psychological Monographs,* 74 (12 Whole No. 499).

Vithal Rao S. Yadav (1988). Family size and order of birth as correlates of the personality dimension. *Indian Journal of Community Guidance and Service,* Vol. 5, No. 3, Sep. 1978.

Von Winterfeldt and Edwards (1986). Adolescent women's contraceptive decision making. *Journal of Health and Social Behavior,* 1991, Vol. 32, pp. 130-44.

Vroom (1964). Decision theory and occupational choice: Some longitudinal data. Peter Harriot Russel Ecob and Maureen. *Journal of Occupation Psychology.* 1980, 53, p. 223.

Waite Barbara, T. Gansender, Bruce and Ratella Robert, J. (1990). A sport specific measure of self acceptance. *Journal of Sports and Exercise Psychology*, Vol. 12(3), pp. 264-79.

Wallach M.A. and Leggett, M.I. (1972). Testing the hypothesis that a person will be consistent:Stylic consistency versus situational specificity in size of children's drawings. *Journal of Personality*, Vol. 40, pp. 309-30.

Watson, J.B. and Raynor, R. (1920). Conditioned emotional responses. *Journal of Experimental Psychology*, 1920, 3, pp. 1-14.

Watson, D. (1967). Relationship between locus of control and anxiety. *Journal of Personality and Social Pscyhology*, Vol. 6, pp. 91-92.

Weiner, B. (1972). *Theories of Motivation*, Chicago. Markham.

Wine, J. (1971). Test anxiety and direction of attention. *Psychological Bullein,* 76, pp. 92-104.

Yerkes, R.M. and Dodson, J.D. (1908). The relation of strength of stimulus to rapidity of habit formation. *Journal of Comparative Neurological Psychology*, 18, pp. 459-82.

Zajonc, R.B. and N.K. Wahi (1961). Conformity and need achievement under cross cultural norm conflict. *Hum. Realt.* 14, pp. 241-50.

Zamft Hyman (1975). Micro Films 36/08 A.P.4956 DCJ.76-04161

Zander, A. and Wolfe, D. (1964). Administrative rewards and Coordination among committee members. *Administrative Science,* 9, pp. 50-69.

Zmud, R.W. (1979). Individual differences in MIS success. A review of the empirical Literature. *Management Science,* 25, pp. 966-79.

Zuckerman, S. and Wheeler, L (1975). To dispel fantacies about the fantacy based measure of fear of success. *Psychological Bulletin.* 82, pp. 932-946.

Index